Our Eternal Contemporary

Our
Eternal Contemporary

*A Study of
the Present-Day Significance of Jesus*

WALTER MARSHALL HORTON
OBERLIN COLLEGE

New York : London
HARPER & BROTHERS PUBLISHERS

To Karl Heim

Contents

Preface

I am dedicating this book to Karl Heim for a very special reason. In Holy Week, 1938, just after the Austrian *Anschluss*, I gave a series of addresses to laymen in Pittsfield, Massachusetts, on the significance of Jesus. These addresses (afterward repeated with variations before student groups in Australia and India, where I went later on that same year, to attend the Madras missionary meeting) formed the original nucleus of this book; and *they were directly inspired by the reading of Karl Heim's two great books,* "*Jesus der Herr*" *and* "*Jesus der Weltvollender.*" (Those who are familiar with these books will recognize that my distinction between Jesus as Leader, as Savior, and as Victor corresponds very closely to Heim's distinction between *Jesus as Führer,* as *Versöhner,* and as *Weltvollender.*)

After finishing the addresses in Pittsfield, I sat down and wrote Heim a letter of gratitude for the inspiration that had come to me from his books, and which I hoped had been in some degree passed on through me to the group of Christian laymen who had heard my addresses. In this letter, as nearly as I can remember, I used these words: "Your country seems to be embarking upon a Napoleonic career which will probably bring it into conflict with mine. If and when that occurs, I want you to know that I shall still be united to you in Christ, though divided from you by war." I never got a reply to the letter, and do not know that it ever got to him through the Nazi censorship; but now that war *has* come between my country and his, I take this opportunity of broadcasting to him publicly (wherever he may be) the message I perhaps failed to communicate to him in private.

I hereby reaffirm, Karl Heim, in the midst of war, that we are one in Christ. The bond between us is something stronger than that of a pleasant friendship, begun in Oberlin, and resumed in your lovely garden by the river in Tübingen. It is the bond of a common loyalty to Jesus Christ, as the One who alone has absolute authority to rule (*Führervollmacht*); before whom all earthly Führers, Presidents, and governments must eventually bow the knee, recognizing that their power is subordinate to His.

My theology is not identical with yours; I cannot for example agree with your conception of Satan. My political views are quite different from yours; I cannot see as much relative good as you see in the Nazi revolution. But we both have the same faith in the supreme authority and saviorhood of God in Christ, and we both try to make our theology and politics interpret this faith. You may not like this book altogether, but you will see in it a tribute to the Lord you serve, and so will not object to the dedication. You may not like to hear that I hope your country will be defeated in this war, but I so hope because I believe it will be better for Christ's cause, better for all God's children, including the German people, that your Führer should be defeated and deposed than that he should be allowed to dominate the world and dictate an "Aryan" peace.

I hope, dear Dr. Heim, that this message will somehow reach you, if you are still living. I long for the day when we may meet again in Oberlin or Tübingen, and collaborate in working for a world order that will give approximate justice to all peoples, including yours and mine, and be more after the Mind of Christ than the world anarchy that now prevails.

The actual writing of this book began when I was invited by the Pacific School of Religion to deliver three Earl Lectures at Berkeley, California, February 20–22, 1940. Chapters ii, iii, and iv of the present version are the Earl Lectures as then presented, but with numerous emendations. The unemended text had been sent to Argentina for translation, soon after it was written, and was read in Spanish as part of a series of lectures I gave at the Facultad Evangelica de Teología, Buenos Aires, in July, 1940. The greater part of chapters i and v consists of additional material first prepared for delivery at the Ministers' Institute, Union Theological Seminary, New York, in July, 1941. This additional material is now at last reduced to writing, after another year of intermittent work upon it.

My thanks are due to President Arthur Cushman McGiffert, Jr., and his colleagues of the Pacific School of Religion for many courtesies afforded, and many valuable criticisms offered at the time of the delivery of the Earl Lectures; to Dr. B. Foster Stockwell of the

Facultad Evangelica, Buenos Aires, for arranging for the Spanish version; to many ministers in New York and elsewhere, who gave their frank reaction on hearing me present these lectures in part or as a whole; to the editors of *Religion in Life, Current Religious Thought,* and the *Journal of Bible and Religion* for allowing me to reprint portions of chapters i and v and Appendix B, which first appeared in their columns; and to the following publishing houses, for permission to quote from their publications: The Macmillan Company; Willett, Clark and Company; the International Missionary Council.

I wish particularly to thank two New Testament scholars, of rather different schools of interpretation, for reading my manuscript and giving me their frank judgments upon it. They are Dr. F. C. Grant of Union Theological Seminary and my own colleague, Dr. Clarence Tucker Craig. They must not be held responsible for my views, as I have not seen fit to accept all their criticisms, but I have benefited from them greatly. Perhaps I might have benefited still more if I had consulted them earlier, before my thought got organized in set patterns, hard to rearrange! One thing is sure, that all my subsequent work in theology is going to be affected by the fresh insight into the meaning of the New Testament which has come to me from this study.

Burlington, Vermont
July 17, 1942

WALTER MARSHALL HORTON

Introduction

The Moratorium on Christology

THERE HAS been something like a general moratorium on the doctrine of Christ in American religious thought for the past quarter century. This has been by no means an unproductive period in American theology; but our most productive and influential writers seem to have avoided the subject of the Person and Work of Christ as if it were taboo. What few books on the subject have appeared in this country have been written by authors born and trained abroad, where discussion of the doctrine of Christ has never ceased.[1] What is the reason for this strange conspiracy of silence among American Christian thinkers, concerning a subject which lies near the very heart of Christianity? As I see it, there are two principal reasons:

1. A generation ago, up to and including the opening years of the First World War, American religious

---

[1] E.g., John Baillie, *The Place of Jesus Christ in Modern Christianity* (1929), and W. Douglas Mackenzie, *The Christ of the Christian Faith* (1933). Both authors were born and educated in Scotland.

thought was deeply affected by *the influence of the Ritschlian theology*. There was a natural kinship between Ritschl's teaching, with its strong ethical-social emphasis, and the dominant characteristics of American Protestantism, so that Ritschlianism "took" in this country as nowhere else in the world. The religious Pragmatism of William James and the Social Gospel of Walter Rauschenbusch were two parallel movements in which the prevalent "activism" of the American mind expressed itself, and these native movements united with the influence of Ritschlianism to form a stable chemical compound that resisted disintegration for a long time.

Now the Ritschlian theology put a taboo upon Christological thought at two important points, compensating for this by an exaggerated and dangerous emphasis at another point. It denounced as "metaphysical" all speculations concerning the pre-existent divine Word who became incarnate in Jesus, or concerning the relationship of Jesus' divine nature to his human nature; and it denounced as "mystical" all alleged experiences of the "Living Christ" whereby modern Christians have claimed to enter into direct personal contact with their Lord and Redeemer. Having thus rejected the greater part of traditional Christology, Ritschl's theology then proceeds to lay furious stress upon what remains, and thereby betrays itself into assertions quite as extreme as its negations. Jesus' metaphysical divinity being excluded even from discussion, his divinity in the pragmatic sense is asserted in the most unqualified terms. He has "the value of God" for us, because in him (i.e., in

the historical figure, Jesus of Nazareth) we find everything we have a right to seek in God: complete "victory
over the world." While we cannot claim to have mystical
contact with our Lord, we can have something better:
moral unity with him, as we take for our "self-end"
that same blessed Will of God which perfectly inspired
every word and deed of his life. The sum of all wisdom,
all inspiration, all deity, is concentrated in those few
short months of his recorded ministry. The God we cannot find in nature, we adore in the human Jesus. "Jesuolatry" was never pushed to greater lengths.

I hope to show, in the chapters that follow — especially in the chapter on "Jesus as Leader" — a proper
appreciation for the truth in the Ritschlian position. I believe that Jesus is indeed, as the Ritschlians contended,
the supreme Prophet of all mankind, the One who definitely revealed the Will of God in word and deed, the
effective Founder on earth of God's eternal Kingdom.
But the Ritschlians presented this truth in the form of a
particular portrait of the historical Jesus, the so-called
"liberal Jesus," in whose historical figure they found
perfectly exemplified all the values cherished by liberal
Christians; and this portrait has now been irretrievably
condemned by New Testament criticism, as a spurious
modernization which falsifies the Great Master it pur-
ports to represent.

The Ritschlians had themselves appealed to New
Testament criticism to confirm the authenticity of their
portrait. They were confident that when all later ac-
cretions, all metaphysical varnish and mystical paint

attributable to later generations had been removed, the resultant portrait of the real historical Jesus would be one in which the ethical faith of the modern man would find its perfect object of devotion. The results have been not at all as predicted. A Jesus-portrait from which all traces of retouching by the Christian community have been scraped away turns out to be nothing like the "liberal Jesus" — in fact, it turns out to be so full of gaps and bare spots that it is next to nothing at all!

To a Christian faith that is not morbidly sensitive about the distinction between "the religion *of* Jesus" and "the religion *about* Jesus," this is no very terrifying discovery. After all, it has generally been recognized that each evangelist, each New Testament writer, saw his Master through a characteristically different pair of spectacles; and thus it is not likely that anything in the New Testament is utterly free from subjectivism. But the Ritschlians *were* morbidly sensitive about this distinction. They believed it could be proved that the religion *of* Jesus (i.e., the religion he practiced himself) was very different from the metaphysical and mystical religion *about* Jesus (i.e., the faith centering in devotion to Christ) which admittedly appears in the New Testament as early as the Epistles of Paul. So when it proved impossible to isolate the "simple ethical religion of Jesus" from the metaphysical and mystical faith of the New Testament church, the Ritschlians suddenly lost all interest in Christology, and turned elsewhere — to philosophy, psychology, and general history, for example — to find a new basis for their shattered faith. This, I think, is the main reason why so many of our American religious thinkers are shy and evasive on the subject of Christology. In their youth, they put their money in the Ritschlian bank, and the bank failed. Since it was New Testament criticism that brought about the crash, they hesitate to make *any* theological affirmations now which could possibly come into collision with New Testament criticism. This makes it impossible for them to say much of anything about Christ.

2. But there is another reason for the moratorium. In the past two decades American theology has been *preoccupied with other urgent problems*, which have drawn attention away from Christology. During the "Jazz Decade" that followed the Armistice, the inherited moral and religious capital of America began to be squandered at a ruinous rate, and atheism began to increase rapidly. In this emergency, American theology became so preoccupied with the primary question of the bases of theistic belief that all secondary questions tended to be shelved. What point was there in discussing the deity of Christ, when the existence of any deity whatsoever was being called in question? More recently, the problem of God has been succeeded by the problem of man, as the center of theological interest. The World Depression and the Second World War have so shaken modern man's faith in himself that a second intellectual emergency has arisen, and speedy theological first aid has again been needed, lest this deepening sense of self-distrust should lead modern man

to nihilism and despair, instead of to a salutary act of repentance. Again, Christology has had to wait.

Now I believe it has waited long enough, and it is time to declare the moratorium at an end. The Ritschlian fight is long over now, and those who were wounded in it have had time to recover. New Testament criticism has ceased to play a purely negative role, so that theology need no longer fear to come into contact with it. And those theological questions with which we have lately been preoccupied have led us back, by a long detour, to the point where the Christological question must be faced. We have discussed the nature of God and the nature of man; next in order, unless we dodge it, is the question of *the right relationship between God and man.* This *is* the Christological problem, for *Christ is the Christian answer to the age-old problem of right relationship between God and man.* And in the present desperate crisis of human history, this question must not, cannot be dodged.

The issue of the hour is no longer, "Is there a God?" or "What is Man?" but "Christ or Antichrist?" The man on the street senses that well enough; he avidly reads popular apocalyptic literature about the loosing of Satan, Gog and Magog, and the coming battle of Armageddon. If sound theology will not speak to him of Christ and Antichrist, he will get him an unsound theology. But some doctrine of Christ he must have, for he instinctively feels that Christ and the Adversary confront him in a most personal way at this historic hour, and require him to choose between them. Theologians ought to admit the reality of this issue which the man in the street faces, and ought to give a careful, considered answer to it.

I have long been troubled about the moratorium on Christology. As one brought up in an evangelical church, where the doctrine of the Living Christ was a cardinal essential of the faith, I was never content with the Ritschlian denial of it. My first published article in the field of theology was entitled "Shall We Discard the Living Christ?" and my answer, with all due critical qualifications, was a definite No. In both of my attempts to sketch the outlines of Christian theology as a whole,[2] I have given central place to the doctrine of Christ. But hitherto, I have judged that the times were not opportune for a fuller treatment of this great theme.

Now, the times are opportune. The moratorium is at an end. This past year (1941) two books have appeared which prove that the "lid is off" at last. I refer to John Knox's little classic, *The Man Christ Jesus*, the most theologically constructive utterance that has come from an American New Testament critic in over a generation, and *Christ and Christian Faith*, by Norman Pittenger, a straight theological discussion by one who has for years been revolving the doctrine of Christ in his mind, during the great silence.[3]

[2] *A Psychological Approach to Theology* (1931) and *Realistic Theology* (1934).

[3] I do not mean of course to suggest that New Testament critics have been uniformly destructive in their attitude to the figure of Jesus. Such a book as Harvie Branscomb's textbook on *The Teachings of Jesus* (1931) contains all that any fair-minded theologian could

The present book is offered as one more contribution to what I hope may be a considerable body of literature, before this decade shall have run its course. It is expressed for the most part in nontechnical language, for it is my hope that this presentation of the heart of the Christian Gospel may be intelligible to laymen as well as to the clergy, and meet their need for a fresh statement of the "old, old story." My experience in speaking to laymen along these lines encourages me in this hope. But this Introduction is addressed to theologians and to the clergy, lest they should be in any doubt as to my theological aims.

---

ask as a historical foundation for faith in Christ. But the total effect of recent New Testament criticism has been to obscure the figure of Jesus in a dense fog of controversy; so Knox's little book renders a great service by allowing the face of the Master to appear clearly once more, in all its human simplicity and superhuman majesty.

Our Eternal Contemporary

Chapter One

Our Eternal Contemporary

I. *The Bible as an eternally contemporary Book*

THE MOST impressive religious drama I have ever seen was *The Eternal Road*, a pageant of Jewish history and destiny written by Franz Werfel, and produced by Max Reinhardt.

Mechanically speaking, the unique effect of this great pageant depends upon the use of a double, or in a sense a multiple, stage.

When the curtain first rises there is disclosed on the lower stage the interior of a modern synagogue, "somewhere in Europe." Here the Jewish inhabitants of a modern city have sought temporary shelter from a mob — whose ominous roar and clamor can from time to time be heard outside — until definite word shall come to them concerning the fate which the Tyrant of that unnamed land has decreed for them. They have a long night of danger and suspense ahead of them. To keep their courage up, the Rabbi brings forth the scroll of Torah, and begins to recall to their minds the great tribulations and divine deliverances of the ancient Hebrews.

As the Rabbi begins to read, a vast upper stage unfolds, on which the sacred story is enacted, while lights are dimmed on the lower stage. This upper stage is built on four levels. The more human and mundane episodes in the narrative — Jacob and Rachel, Israel in Egypt, the Golden Calf, the dance of the reapers in the story of Ruth — are enacted on the lower levels, while the uppermost level, known as the "Gate of Heaven," is reserved for the decisive moments of divine-human interaction, such as the sacrifice of Isaac and the receiving of the Tables of the Law. Winding upward from depth to height, connecting the lower stage of modernity with the upper stage of sacred history, connecting all the divine-human levels of sacred history with one another, and tapering off to a vanishing point at the Gate of Heaven, is a road ("The Eternal Road") symbolizing the unity of destiny which binds the ancient Hebrew and the modern Jew together.

This unity of destiny becomes more and more manifest as the play proceeds. At first, what happens on the upper stage appears to be only an ancient story; then the ancient story begins to be mysteriously linked with the fate of modern Jewry.

During one of the interludes, when the light shifts back to the lower stage and the contemporary drama is resumed, a skeptic creates an uproar in the synagogue by ridiculing the religious faith of his compatriots. He declares that the perpetual sufferings of the Jews are due principally to the fact that they have gone through history carrying a mountain on their backs — a mountain whose name is "God." Now for his part he proposes to cast that mountain off! Amid cries of horror and reproach he leaves the synagogue — only to appear a few moments later in the next episode of the ancient story, above! He is the leader of the grumbling and refractory Israelites who complain against Moses during the march through the Wilderness, sigh for the fleshpots of Egypt, and set up the Golden Calf when Moses tarries too long with the Lord, upon the summit of Sinai. Later, he reappears in other episodes — tempting David to sin with Bathsheba, or sneering at the prophecies of Jeremiah. He is the Eternal Skeptic, the Eternal Adversary, everlastingly leading Israel to fall away from God, and so to fall into disaster. (I may add that he is a recognizable modern type. I have met him at Columbia University.)

Another effective linkage between the lower and upper stages occurs when two new refugees arrive in the synagogue, a young Jew and his Gentile wife. The congregation is alarmed at her presence, for she is related to some of their chief persecutors, and her husband urges her to seek safety with her kin; but she refuses to leave him and wishes to share the fate of his people, whatever it may be. The Rabbi, appealed to for a decision in this difficult case, answers by reading the opening words of the Book of Ruth, which is then enacted above. Once again, ancient and modern events become parallel windings of one Eternal Road, as Ruth the

Moabitess re-echoes the words of the modern Gentile girl: "Entreat me not to leave thee or to return from following after thee; for whither thou goest I will go; and where thou lodgest I will lodge; thy people shall be my people, and thy God my God."

At the end, the parallelism becomes complete identity. The ancient Hebrews go forth, lamenting, into the Babylonian Exile; while the modern Jews go forth at dawn from the synagogue, stunned by a message from the Tyrant ordering them to leave the country within twenty-four hours. The two streams of exiles, ancient and modern, find themselves mingling together, walking side by side on the same Eternal Road. They are one in their sorrows, but they are one in their hopes, too; for as they go forth a high, youthful voice is raised in their midst: "King Messiah . . . I see you . . . I hear you . . . !" It is the voice of a thirteen-year-old modern boy, the son of an estranged Jew, who had never heard the story of his people until he heard and saw the whole of it in one synoptic view, this memorable night. It is all news to him — Good News. His fresh, boyish eyes see the coming liberation already, while his elders see only the beginning of the exile. In response to his cry of faith, ancient and modern Israel burst out together into a psalm of hope: "When the Lord brought the exiles back to Zion, we were as those that dream. Then were our mouths filled with laughter and our tongues with singing."

II. Jesus as the eternally contemporary Man

What the authors of *The Eternal Road* so convincingly demonstrate concerning the Jewish Bible — that it spans the gulf between ancient and modern times — Christians believe to be even truer of the Christian Bible and of its central figure, Jesus of Nazareth. As the Bible is an eternally contemporary Book, Jesus is the eternally contemporary Man. What Max Reinhardt has so effectively suggested by the dramatic device of a double stage and a connecting road, contemporary Christian writers have endeavored to suggest by a variety of literary and dramatic devices. Francis Thompson gave us the model for many such attempts when, in an unforgettable line, he showed us Christ "walking on the waters, not of Gennesaret, but Thames." So Stanley Jones, in a whole series of books, has shown us Christ walking "the Indian road" and "every road" as our ever-present contemporary; Richard Roberts, in another series, has shown us *That One Face* reflected in the greatest poets and prophets of Christendom, from Dante and Savonarola to the Victorian Age, until at last it looks out upon us from the issues of our own days, as the face of *The Contemporary Christ;* Ricardo Rojas, in *The Invisible Christ*, has followed that same Face through the bewildering varieties of Christian iconography, and found its Original at last nót in some ancient authentic portrait of the Nazarene, but in a living contemporary Presence, crowned again with thorns by our godless modern civilization, but ready to redeem our world as he redeemed the ancient world if we permit him to be reborn in us today.

There must be truth in the idea of Jesus as *Our Eternal Contemporary*, when writers of so many different shades of opinion try with one accord to convey this same idea by such divergent technical devices. Consider for example two very striking recent dramatizations of the life of Jesus: *Family Portrait*, a three-act play by Lenore Coffee and William Joyce Cowen, and *The Nazarene*, a narrative of epic proportions by the Yiddish novelist, Sholem Asch. The former aims to shatter the complacency of modern conventional Christians; the latter, to stir the interest of modern pagans and modern Jews; but both create the impression that the Man of Nazareth is as much alive and as truly present to our generation as to his own.

Sholem Asch brings this home to his readers by the somewhat violent literary device of a supposed *reincarnation* on the part of his two principal narrators. The authors of *Family Portrait* accomplish the same result more simply, by a kind of *deliberate anachronism* in the dialogue and setting. As the old masters painted the Holy Family in the dress and environment of the late Middle Ages, these modern American playwrights portray a not-so-holy family in a Nazareth which might be in the State of Pennsylvania. When these American Nazarenes — recognizable contemporary types, even to the round collar and priggish clerical mannerisms of James, the hyper-Pharisee of the family — when these conventional modern Christians begin to comment, in

the idiom of twentieth-century America, upon the
scandalous behavior of their brother Jesus, the effect is
devastating and revealing.

Both in the American play and the Yiddish novel,
Jesus is presented as a living enigma too fascinating to
be dropped, but too profound or too simple to be
solved, save by a venturesome life decision, for him [1]
or against him. In both, the contrasting figures of Judas
Iscariot and Mary Magdalene stand out as embodiments
of two eternal alternatives; and we find in ourselves an
appalling ability to *understand* Judas, while we only
wonder at Mary. The extraordinary claims and promises
of the Nazarene embarrass us, disturb us, as only a living
contemporary can embarrass or disturb us.

III. The meaning of "eternally contemporary"

What is the truth about the Bible and about Jesus of
Nazareth, which inspires so many different writers to
assert or suggest that this Book and this Man, unlike
other books and other men, are *eternally contemporaneous* with every passing generation, and will continue

[1] It is customary to spell pronouns referring to Jesus with a capital
H, as a mark of reverence. Since we shall be referring to Jesus constantly in this book, and since the question how and why we should
revere him is the very question we are discussing, it seems best
as a rule to spell all pronouns referring to him with a modest *h*,
unless there is some special reason to do otherwise. Ordinarily, then,
we shall use small letters when referring to Jesus of Nazareth, the
historical character, but when we refer to Jesus as God's incarnate
Word, we shall use capitals. There is a kind of effusive reverence
which Jesus himself found very obnoxious (Luke 11:27, 28; 18:18, 19).
Let us not fall into it even in spelling.

to be so "even unto the end of the world?" Just how literally can such assertions be taken? What precisely do they mean? It is not necessary for dramatists and novelists to trouble themselves with these questions, but it is necessary for religious thinkers to face them clearly; for it is the purpose of religion, even when it uses the language of poetry and devotion, to express reality, and not merely to evoke appreciative feeling. What is the reality to which the "Eternal Road," the "Invisible Christ," and similar symbolic expressions all bear witness? It may be well to approach this reality step by step, beginning with assertions that are certainly true, and pushing out beyond these truisms to the bolder assertions of religious faith if the reality itself requires us to take this further step.

1. *The Bible is a classic, and like other classics is eternally contemporary*. This is a truism to which all literate people might subscribe. Most writings are ephemeral, and speak only to their own time. There is a rapid turnover in such writings, as in popular slang and popular music. The book-of-the-month or the book-of-the-year seldom turns out to be the book-of-the-century, and even the book-of-the-century seldom is intelligible or interesting to other centuries. The Bible is one of those perennial classics which have survived their own age and been admitted to literary immortality. Books which achieve this rank are no longer mere products of a particular state of culture; they are culture-making and culture-sustaining forces, as the Confucian Classics have been in China for over two thousand years. When

they are neglected, the culture languishes; when they are freshly related to contemporary needs, the culture revives; if they are wholly set aside, without being replaced by new "books of power," the culture dies, and only a new set of classics can bring it to life again. Let American culture, which was founded on the Bible and has forgotten the Bible, take note!

2. *The Bible is not only a Jewish classic, or a Western classic, but a universal human classic, speaking to the condition of all men in all times, with contemporary relevance.* This is a truth which in the nature of the case can never be completely demonstrated, but it is in process of demonstration. Every time the Bible is translated into a new language, and its message finds response in a new environment, something is added to the huge mass of evidence tending to show that it belongs to mankind as a whole. I would defy any Gentile to witness such a Biblical pageant as *The Eternal Road* without saying to himself, "This Road with many windings — bondage and liberation, exile and homecoming, oppression and deliverance, many times repeated — surely it is not the Jews only who must tread it. We too must wander in Wildernesses, and seek Promised Lands; we too miss happiness in our Promised Lands when we arrive there, and must pass through new disciplines in exile before we are fit to return again. The Eternal Road of the Jews is the Eternal Road of mankind." I know there are many individuals and not a few nations in the world today who would make no such response, and scornfully reject the idea that they ever might do

so. But in the light of past reversals, I would say to them, "Wait and see. See if your sons do not return to the classic you have rejected, like the Estranged One's son in the pageant. See if your nation, having played the role of the Eternal Skeptic for a time, does not turn again at the next bend in the road of destiny, and come back to slake its thirst at the old springs. In every endurance contest between the Bible and those who despise it, the odds are on the Bible."

3. *Jesus of Nazareth stands at the culminating point of that line of decisive divine acts which gives the Bible its timeless quality and its unified meaning.* The Old Testament gets its unity from the fact that whenever the Children of Israel turn back to the Lord in humility and faith, they are saved from the evils that surround them; and when these saving acts of God — which Max Reinhardt significantly sets upon a higher stage-level than other events, at the very Gate of Heaven — when these acts are arranged in sequence, they form a meaningful whole, a "plan of salvation," interrupted by comparatively futile and trivial episodes of human wandering and willfulness. Not everything in the Old Testament is in itself of eternal significance, but this chain of divinely meaningful events confers eternal contemporaneity upon everything connected with it, as though it involved a veritable incursion of the eternal into the temporal.

At the end, however, the chain is broken. The Messianic hope in which the faith of Israel culminates is an unfulfilled hope, a prayer without an answer. In the person of Jesus, the vacant role of Messiah is more than filled, and the prayer is more than answered, if the faith of Christendom be not mistaken. It is only by faith that any event is recognized as an act of God, and this applies to the events commemorated by Christians at Christmas, Good Friday, and Easter as to the events commemorated by Jews at their Passover and Purim festivals; but such faith at its best is never groundless. When Christian faith sees Jesus as the fulfiller of Old Testament prophecy and *the* decisive Act of God in history, the empirical ground of this faith is the fact that through Jesus and his followers the eternal and universal elements in Judaism were disentangled from its transient and local elements, and made available for all mankind. It is principally through its connection with the New Testament that the Old Testament has become a world classic. By itself, it is still a classic, but of a more limited appeal.

4. *Jesus is our Eternal Contemporary in a higher and more mysterious sense than any that can be predicated of a Book*. It is often said of him that he is to the Christian "what Torah is to the Jew." That is, Christians look to him when they wish to know the Word and Will of God, just as Jews look to the Law. But they look in a different way. The highest assertion the Jews have ever made about the Law of Moses is that it was *written by* the Eternal Wisdom of God, the "breath of the power of God," [2] whereby He made heaven and

[2] Wisdom of Solomon 7:25; cf. Prov. 3:19, Wisdom of Sirach 24:3 ff.

earth; and through pondering its commandments, one might rise to the knowledge of its Author. Christians have made a bolder assertion about Jesus: that he *is* himself "the power of God and the wisdom of God." [3] In him, so to speak, the Author of the Bible (yes, and of all creation) has appeared in person, to interpret the meaning of His work. If even in the pages of an ancient Book, full of references to vanished nations and forgotten events, we may from time to time hear God speaking to us directly, how much more directly must God speak to us — at every time and place — through him who *embodies* the divine Wisdom that is "the fashioner of all things," "penetrates and permeates everything," and is "a spotless mirror of the activity of God . . . a likeness of his goodness." [4]

It is difficult to state all that Christian faith means to imply by this last stupendous affirmation. The life of Jesus shades off into mystery, whether we consider its ultimate source or its ultimate outcome. Perhaps the best way to interpret the meaning of faith in Jesus as "the power and wisdom of God" is simply to point to the mysteries that surround his life and his influence.

[3] I Cor. 1:24.

[4] Wisdom of Solomon 7:22, 24, 26 (Goodspeed's translation). Sholem Asch in his illuminating book *What I Believe* (pp. 107, 108) calls attention to the peculiar and personal directness with which Jesus spoke to his Jewish contemporaries on behalf of God — an assumption of divine authority which led to his rejection. He spoke not as an *expositor* of Moses and the prophets, remarks Asch, but with "the tongue of the power" whereby the Law was delivered to Moses. And furthermore, he not only thought of himself as carrying the mandate; he considered himself part of the mandate.

(1) Jesus came forth not merely from his people and his time, but came forth, as it were, *to* his people, to his time, from the eternal world that lies beyond the Gate of Heaven — a human figure issuing forth from that inviolable frontier behind which the Lord God hides His glory, and from which hitherto had issued only momentary visions and voices, commands and promises. (2) When he vanished again from his contemporaries, he did not leave them bereft of his companionship. The eternal life which he brought with him into the plane of time remained with his followers as the gift of his Spirit and still remains as a promise of greater things to come. (3) When we look to him out of our present distresses, and cry to him for help, we do not raise our voices, as though two thousand years of time and change, or as though some unbridgeable gulf, parting time and eternity, stood between us. The one to whom we cry seems to be at the same time our living contemporary and our eternal link with the unchanging God. He is "the same yesterday, today, and forever" — and because of him the world is forever different. He is with us, because the eternal world where he dwells is immediately present to every moment of time; and he is with us, because his Spirit has never ceased to walk the earth and share our human vicissitudes, since first he looked with compassion upon the woes of men in Nazareth.

All this, of course, is a daring venture of Christian faith, whose full validity we cannot assume at the beginning of our study, but must proceed to test. Perhaps we cannot expect to prove this faith in its whole audacious sweep; that would be like measuring Heaven with a foot rule. But if it should turn out, as we proceed, that Jesus is still for us today what he was for some of his historic contemporaries — Leader, Savior, and Victor — then would this not tend to indicate that this persistent Christian postulate of faith was justified, and he was indeed our Eternal Contemporary? Surely no dead teacher could lead us now, no ancient prophet could save us, no spent force could give us victory over the hosts of darkness that now beset us! Only the eternal God, made manifest through His eternal Word of Wisdom, could thus deliver us. If Jesus can deliver us, he must indeed be "the power of God and the wisdom of God."

IV. Our knowledge of Jesus: historical criticism and Christian faith

Our method of testing the presence of God's power and wisdom in Jesus is first to set his figure realistically over against his historic contemporaries, and then consider whether his significance is exhausted in his relationship to them, or whether his words and deeds come home to us powerfully and relevantly across the centuries, as if addressed to us. In following out this method, we shall have to take care not to attribute our own modern views and attitudes to Jesus, and then proceed to extract them from him again, like a magician pulling a rabbit out of a hat. This procedure has been all too prevalent among Christian preachers and teachers. Our great protection against it is *New Testament criticism.*

New Testament criticism is a special branch of historical criticism, whose purpose everywhere and always is to see to it that historical events be narrated just as they happened, historical documents allowed to mean just what they originally meant, and historical characters made to stand for just what they originally stood for, no matter how many interesting and valuable meanings have subsequently become attached to them.[5] Historical criticism is particularly necessary when we are dealing with classical books and great characters, for, as we have seen, such books and such men have the power to outlive their time and take on new meanings for every subsequent generation. When these later meanings accumulate and become hallowed by sacred associations, they often come to encrust the original meaning so deeply that it is practically hidden from view. It is then the business of the historical critic to scrape away these incrustations, however excellent they may be in their own way, and reveal the underlying historical facts.

In the interest of religion as well as in the interest of historical veracity, this needs to be done. If the Bible is

[5] In its study of the New Testament, historical criticism operates at four successive levels: "first comes Textual Criticism, research of the manuscripts, early quotations, and versions; then Literary Criticism, the study of the finished gospels as they left the hands of their authors; then Source Criticism, by which we endeavor to reconstruct the documents or oral cycles used by the writers; then Form Criticism, the study of the oral tradition as it circulated prior to the writing of any documents, prior even to its incorporation in any cycle or setting, oral or written." (F. C. Grant, *The Gospel of the Kingdom* [The Macmillan Company, 1940], p. 27. Quoted by permission.)

a divinely inspired Book, and Jesus a divinely sent Leader, religious reverence requires that we listen to the Book itself and not to something we have read into it, bow before the Leader himself and not before some legendary man-made image of him. Once we have honestly confronted the original, it may appear that many of the later-added meanings are essentially true to it, and we may be inspired to offer some really new interpretation of its meaning for the modern world; but we are lacking in religious respect, we are presuming to correct God's actual revelation of Himself, if we fail to do our utmost to press back as close as possible to what historians call primary sources. That is what every conscientious preacher does when he looks up the original Greek or Hebrew meaning of his text, and tries to reconstruct its original setting. From such careful, historically critical use of a text the most novel insights into its modern meaning, its eternal meaning, may spring. To neglect historical criticism and indulge in mere homiletical fancies is to be a slovenly "divider" of God's Word of Truth.[6]

In the study of the life and teachings of Jesus, the proper interweaving of faith and criticism is peculiarly difficult, for *it is through the faith of the New Testament Church, and through this medium alone, that we see Jesus at all.* Outside of the Four Gospels and the other New Testament writings, there are practically no documents by which the record can be checked. Both

[6] See Appendix A for further discussion of the relation between historical criticism and Christian faith.

contemporary Jewish literature and contemporary Roman history practically ignore Jesus, and afford at best a background against which his portrait in the Gospels can be set. When criticism attempts to push beyond this portrait to the underlying historical facts, it has to proceed by a difficult and uncertain process of triangulation and hypothesis. In all probability, it will never fully succeed in differentiating between the Jesus of history and the Christ of faith. For a time, it seemed possible to distinguish between the "historical Jesus" of the Synoptic Gospels and the "theological Christ" of Paul and John; but it now seems clear that Mark, though closer to the historical events than the author of the Fourth Gospel, is just as "theological" in his own way, while even the earliest collections of the sayings of Jesus, in "Q" and other sources, are colored by the faith of the Early Church, and artificially arranged for teaching and preaching purposes.

That is not to say that we must despise and set aside whatever is marked by the mentality of the Early Church. *That which Christian faith apprehends as divine in the New Testament is not merely the individual Man Christ Jesus, but a movement of events that begins with him and passes over to his followers.* The word "Christ" in the New Testament connotes both the "mind of Christ" and "spirit of Christ" in the Church and the historical Leader from whom that mind and spirit are believed to be authentically derived. Deviations from the intention of the Leader did of course occur in the Church; but so long as there is vital *continuity* between the animating mind and spirit of the Christian movement and its historic Founder, we find Christ in the Church, and not only in Jesus. That there *is* vital continuity between Jesus and the Church, Porter has shown in *The Mind of Christ in Paul*. What New Testament criticism can give us, then, is *not* a portrait of Jesus wholly clear of Church influence, but a portrait sufficiently close to the original, because drawn from the earliest and most spontaneous faith of the Church, so that it can be used to test the authenticity of later, spuriously modernized Christ-images.

The only doubts that need absolutely to be resolved, before such a portrait of Jesus can be used with a clear conscience, are two: (1) Did Jesus really live? and (2) From the incomplete records of the New Testament, can we know enough of his words and deeds to form a clear, reliable conception of his character and significance? The first of these two doubts strikes at the very center of our Christian faith: the conviction that God is active in history, and His highest revelation is in a real historical character who was "conceived . . . born . . . suffered . . . crucified, dead, and buried," as could never be affirmed of any Greek or Hindu god.[7] The second is like unto the first in its ultimate effect,

[7] It would perhaps be possible to reconcile Christian faith with a skeptical attitude on this question by insisting that God *had* been active in the history of Israel before Christ, and *somewhere in the New Testament era* (if not in Jesus then *in the Church*) there occurred a fresh and lasting outburst of His wisdom and power into human history. Royce's *Problem of Christianity* takes this view. But surely the Church without Jesus is unthinkable. On the significance of the historical element in Christianity. see Appendix B.

for if it is impossible to know anything definite or reliable about the character of Jesus, it is practically as though he had never lived at all, and we had better center our faith upon the clear-cut figures of the prophets and the apostles than upon this nebulous blur that lies between them.

On the first of these doubts, considerable critical analysis has been expended, and it may now be announced without fear of serious contradiction that the so-called "mythical" view of Jesus, whether in its nineteenth-century form (D. F. Strauss) or in its twentieth-century form (Drews, W. B. Smith, etc.), is itself as purely mythical as the myth of Aryan racial purity and superiority, with which it has sometimes been associated. Jesus certainly lived and certainly was crucified under Pontius Pilate, about the year 30 of our era: that is sober history, practically incontrovertible.[8] But was he a significant character, great and unique enough to bear the weight of God's central historic work of redemption, which Christian faith has always placed upon his shoulders? The importance of John Knox's recent book, *The Man Christ Jesus*, lies in its frank and thorough facing of this question. We may agree with him that a negative answer to it would be a practical denial of the

[8] The shortest way to establish the historicity of Jesus is first to establish the unquestionable authenticity of the major epistles of Paul, and then note the fact that Paul conversed with James the brother of Jesus when he went up to Jerusalem to meet the "pillars of the Church." (Gal. 1:19.) See Branscomb, *The Teachings of Jesus*, chap. i, for a brief summary of all the evidence which assures the historicity of Jesus, including the extra-Biblical testimony of Tacitus, Josephus, etc.

historicity of Jesus, for it would "so reduce his stature or change his aspect that it ceases to matter whether he lived or not." [9]

The acclaim with which some of our severest New Testament critics have greeted Knox's portrait of the character of Jesus is a very hopeful sign. It means that there actually exists more of a consensus among competent critics with regard to the *general outlines* of Jesus' life and work than the bewildered public has sometimes supposed. The conflicts of opinion which have hidden the figure of Jesus, and made theologians turn away from the Gospels in despair to take refuge in modern philosophy, ancient prophecy, or Reformation theology, are proved to be mostly conflicts over minor details, which may run their course indefinitely without obscuring the distinctive traits of Jesus' character.[10]

[9] Knox, *op. cit.*, p. 15. (Willett, Clark, 1941.)

[10] *More* than John Knox and other careful New Testament critics are willing to say about the historical Man Christ Jesus, Christian faith does not require as the foundation of its most stupendous utterances about the Christ of God. In all that follows, we presuppose that Jesus was very much as Knox describes him. In such a Man, God could and we believe did accomplish, for the modern world as well as for the ancient, all that is most necessary for the world's redemption: pointed the Way through his Leadership, "slew the enmity" through his forgiving love, inflicted a decisive defeat upon the forces of evil through his victorious humiliation, and founded a new humanity through the sacrament of his broken body and shed blood. It is not necessary to despoil all peoples of their characteristic virtues and values, and load those excellences upon the figure of Jesus; nor is it necessary to deny that outside of him we have real access to God by many avenues. No more is necessary than this: that his human character should be such as to make it con-

Our attitude toward Biblical criticism and Christian faith should now be clear. We regard them as two equally important but very different sources of knowledge about the real Jesus. The first is precise and accurate but shallow, like scientific knowledge; the second is deep and penetrating, like all knowledge of personal acquaintance and loyal affection, but apt to be inaccurate about details and matters of fact. Ideally, the two should supplement each other in one harmonious portrait; actually, they are always in tension with one another, but do at least help to correct each other. It will be our task in the chapters that follow to weave

---

ceivable that the central line in God's redemptive process should pass through such a one as he.

Less than this, however, is not enough for Christian faith to work with. When certain contemporary theologians, notably Karl Barth, try to combine utter reverence for the unique divine revelation in Jesus Christ with utter indifference to his human character and personality, they attempt the impossible. I agree with John Bennett that the following sentence from Barth is "disparaging" to Jesus; so disparaging, that it logically undermines Barth's faith in Christ as the unique Mediator between God and man: "Jesus Christ in fact is also the Rabbi of Nazareth, historically so difficult to get information about, and when it is got, one whose activity is so easily a little commonplace alongside more than one founder of a religion and even alongside many later representatives of his own religion." (Barth, *The Doctrine of the Word of God*, p. 188, quoted in Bennett, *Christian Realism*, pp. 121–22.) Only the highest of high Calvinists, persuaded that God works "when, where, and how it pleaseth Him" and can reveal Himself in lifeless stocks and stones, if He so choose, rather than in some really congruous medium — only such a mind could be content to find God's decisive revelation in a "commonplace" man. Far better to worship the God of David, or Mohammed, or Oliver Cromwell, who with all their faults were not commonplace men!

the two sorts of knowledge together into one composite account of the Work and the Person of Jesus Christ, as far as this can honestly be done. We start with the conviction, born of personal discipleship to Jesus, that he is our Eternal Contemporary, God's incarnate wisdom and power not only to his own age but to our age as well; and we proceed to test this conviction by casting the actual historical Jesus, the Man of Nazareth as described by historical criticism, in this sublime role. Does he limp pathetically in the part, or does he wear his regal robes as one ordained to rule? That is the test.

V. *The teachings of Jesus: their enduring significance*

The test we have proposed is to be applied to the whole *lifework* of Jesus rather than to his *teachings*. It is a great mistake to think of him as primarily a religious *teacher*, the permanence of whose work is to be judged by the permanent validity of the body of principles and maxims which he bequeathed to mankind.[11] Buddha might fairly be judged by such a criterion, but not Jesus. The Buddha comforted his disciples, when they lamented his approaching death, with the thought that in the Four Noble Truths, and the Noble Eightfold Path, they possessed teachings which would guide them as well in his absence as in his presence. He underestimated the significance of his own person, no doubt; and yet it remains true that he was primarily a teacher, a

[11] Cf. Branscomb, *The Teachings of Jesus*, chap. vi, "Was Jesus Primarily a Teacher?"

discoverer and communicator of truths, while Jesus was
primarily something more than that. The followers of
Jesus would never have been consoled for his death by
their continued possession of his teachings. They looked
for him to come again to complete the work he had
begun to *do,* and they were comforted, while they
waited, by the activity of his living Spirit in their midst.

This, however, should not lead one to minimize the
enduring significance of Jesus' teachings. If the Sermon
on the Mount and the Parables were expunged from the
New Testament record, we should fumble in the dark
for the meaning of the remainder. The character and
mission of Jesus, the direction of the movement which
he founded and led, are largely defined by his teachings. The God he served, the God in obedience to
whose Will he took the way of the Cross, is the God
described in the Sermon and the Parables. We may be
confident that they would not have been put into the
record at all had they not been felt necessary to interpret the meaning of the Christian movement to its sec-
ond-generation members and to the world. The Early
Church traveled light, and carried no excess baggage.
But the importance of the teachings was and is, so to
speak, *adverbial rather than substantive.* That is, the
teachings do not constitute an independent body of
precepts, a set of ethical formulae claiming universal
validity in their own right, like the ethical maxims of
Kant; they simply help to define the direction of the
movement of which Jesus and his apostles were, under
God, the initiators. They modify every essential ac-

tion that enters into this movement — from Jesus' first act of healing in Galilee to Paul's arrival in Rome — as an adverb modifies a verb, defining the manner or spirit in which the action is performed.

The most appropriate way of dealing with the *message* of Jesus is therefore to treat it as incidental to his *mission*, and as an expression of his *character*. That is how we propose to treat it, in the main.[12] But there are important issues connected with Jesus' teaching-mission which need some special attention at the start. The shortest way of summing up these issues is to ask the question, "Are the teachings of Jesus *eternally contemporary*, or are they so determined by local and temporary conditions that they have no value for the modern world?"

It may be assumed without debate that if Jesus was a truly historical character, living under genuinely human conditions — and the stoutest Christian orthodoxy has always insisted upon this — some aspects of his teaching must relate so closely to his own time and the existing situation that they have relatively little value for other times and other situations. There is much, for example, in the debate between Jesus and his opponents over the Law and the Temple which has no more importance for modern Christians than the discussion of "*circumcision*" and "*uncircumcision*" in the Epistles of Paul. These matters were of momentous importance before Judaism and Christianity parted company; since

[12] See, for example, the section on "Whither is Jesus now leading us?" at the end of the next chapter.

then, the changed situation makes them of no great interest or value to modern Christians. In any historical revelation, just because it *is* historical, we must encounter a certain amount of dead wood of this sort. A skillful student of Scripture can often discover analogies between dead issues and living issues, and so rescue large passages of Scripture from superannuation; but all must admit that there are limits to this salvaging process, and some parts of Scripture (including some parts of the teachings of Jesus) are at best like the necessary "roughage" that we all consume with our food. No one is greatly troubled about this, however.

A much more troublesome question has to do with the limitation of Jesus' knowledge concerning the time and manner of the coming of the Kingdom of God. This is no dead issue, like the Law and the Temple, but a matter of vital importance to us, as to him. He himself is quoted as saying, "Concerning that day and hour no man knoweth, no, not the angels which are in heaven, neither the Son, but the Father only." (Mark 13:32.) His authority cannot therefore be cited in favor of those elaborate calculations of dates which have brought so many Adventists to grief. But the whole weight of his authority is nevertheless on the side of a sudden and cataclysmic coming of the Kingdom, some time in the very near future. His disciples certainly expected to see him returning "on the clouds of heaven" during their own lifetime; and though *their* hope, rather than his, may be reflected in such passages as the "little Apocalypse" in Mark 13, it is impossible to explain the universality of this hope in the New Testament Church, and the presence of this hope in all the Gospels, except on the assumption that the Master himself had encouraged it. What becomes of the truth of his teachings, what becomes of his divine mission, one may ask, if he could be so badly mistaken on a matter of such moment?

This issue was artificially sharpened a generation ago by the "consistent eschatology" school of New Testament critics, led by Albert Schweitzer. According to this school, everything in the life of Jesus — his actions and decisions as well as the form and content of his teachings — was determined by his expectation that the world was about to be destroyed and miraculously renewed by divine power. He sent forth his disciples in the expectation that the great tribulation (that was to precede the Time of the End) would overtake them before they had gone through the cities of Palestine. When they returned safely, without experiencing any such hardship or persecution as he had predicted, he concluded that what was yet lacking, before the Kingdom could come, was that he, the Messiah-to-be, should suffer death vicariously on behalf of those who were to inherit the Kingdom, and so ransom them from the power of evil that was temporarily to hold high carnival on earth. If he kept his Messiahship secret, it was because he was not yet Messiah, and would assume that role only *after* his death, *after* the Tribulation, after his return on the clouds of heaven as predicted in the popular dream of the coming of a celestial Son of Man.[13] All that

[13] See Schweitzer, *Out of My Life and Thought,* pp. 51–54, 61, 62.

he did, thought, or said followed "logically" from his acceptance of this popular hope which we find explicitly recorded in such contemporary apocalypses as Enoch, the Psalms of Solomon, Baruch, and Ezra.

Contemporary New Testament scholarship has generally rejected Schweitzer's extreme statement of the case. John Knox summarizes the present consensus in three propositions:

(1) The Kingdom of God, for Jesus, was "not heaven, but the coming reign of righteousness and peace among men to which the prophets looked forward." (2) "Jesus expected momentarily the decisive act of God which would suddenly inaugurate the new age of righteousness and peace. . . . Jesus did not conceive of a long future during which men would 'coöperate' with God in 'building the Kingdom'; such a conception is modern to the core and would have been quite unintelligible to Jesus." In this, he resembled the apocalyptic writers. But (3) the Kingdom was *not* for Jesus, as it was for the apocalyptic writers, "an altogether new and unimaginable order of existence, either in some remote heaven or on an earth so radically changed as to be a new and different earth. . . . The Kingdom of God was to be . . . a fulfilment *within* history . . . within men's hearts and within men's world. . . . In his own words and works, in the life of the little community which had formed about him, the Kingdom had already been manifested." [14]

---

[14] Knox, *op. cit.*, pp. 37–41. Quoted by permission of Willet, Clark and Co., publishers. It ought perhaps to be added that, while Jesus expected the Kingdom to come on this familiar earth, he apparently expected strange things to happen at the inauguration of the New Age; the resurrection of ancient patriarchs and prophets, and the cessation of "marrying and giving in marriage" (Matt. 22:30).

That is to say, there was a strong eschatological element in the teaching of Jesus, looking forward urgently to a great transformation at the end of the age, but his thought and actions were not so completely dominated by this expectation as the "consistent eschatology" school maintained.

One way of conceiving the eschatological element in the teaching of Jesus is to think of it as a passing "thought-form," a temporary intellectual "framework," borrowed from his age, within which and in spite of which his original and lasting insights have been preserved for posterity. I am not satisfied with this view. Part of the unique significance of Jesus, part of his essential insight, is to be seen in his announcement that "the time is fulfilled, and the Kingdom of God is at hand" (Mark 1:15). He did indeed live "in the fullness of the times," in the most critical moment of world history until now; and we who live in another critical time should see in his sense of swift-approaching judgment mingled with great potential good, and repentance as the only way out, something better than a pardonable mistake! The Day of the Lord *did* swiftly come upon his people in the terrible years from A.D. 66 to 70, and the little band of meek and repentant peasants who followed him *did* pass through that great tribulation to "inherit the earth," becoming the acknowledged heroes and leaders of Western civilization down to modern times.

All this we now know as a matter of fact, whereas he saw these coming historical events "through a glass darkly," in terms of mysterious prophetic imagery partly

borrowed from his contemporaries. Our conception of
the Kingdom's coming is inevitably shaped, then, by
our knowledge of the discrepancy between what Jesus
and his disciples expected and what actually occurred;
but our perception of this discrepancy does not destroy
our faith in their prophetic insight. Neither Old Testament prophecy nor New Testament prophecy is dis-
credited or superannuated by mere inexactitude. It is
not characteristic of true prophecy to envisage the
future with photographic precision — God Himself cannot do that, if the future is really contingent to any extent — but rather to survey the possibilities of a particular historical situation in the light of the eternal
counsels of God. There is always an "if" in true prophecy, which makes exact fulfillment improbable, quite
apart from the limitations of the prophet's knowledge of
the situation; but if his understanding of the Will of
God is profound enough, his prophecy for the immediate future may serve innumerable later generations of
men, as they face their own dark future. There are
many today who will testify that nothing helps them
so much to grapple with the problem of human destiny
that darkens our own horizon as to meditate upon the
prophecies of Jesus and his followers, coming as they
do from an age that has the same "apocalyptic" quality
as ours. The precise details of Jesus' prophecies are of
transient significance; the apocalyptic insight that inspired them is of lasting significance.

We have now passed through two layers in the teaching of Jesus, one *obviously transient*, the other *partly*

transient, partly lasting, in its significance. Is there a still deeper layer in them which is *absolutely eternal, always contemporaneous* with every age? I think there is. It is found in Jesus' constant reference of every question to the one supreme criterion of the Will of God, and his interpretation of this Will in terms of a righteousness and a love that are both absolutely without limits. If Jesus' conception of the *time and manner* of the Kingdom's coming needs some restatement in terms of later events, his conception of the *nature* of the Kingdom as that state of affairs where the Will of God is "done on earth as it is in heaven" needs no such restatement. If there are ethical teachings (such as those on paying taxes) which reflect the peculiar relation in which the Jews then stood to their Roman masters, this relativity does not affect the motive from which the particular teachings spring nor the criterion by which they are all tested; i.e., does such and such an act put God's Will first, express God's original intention, or is it corrupted by human conventions and selfish passions?

The Sermon on the Mount is a collection of sayings which in their totality describe the life that is perfectly according to God's Will of universal justice and impartial mercy, irrespective of circumstances. Because circumstances are boldly ignored in all these sayings, the whole Sermon on the Mount will never be perfectly practicable in *any* instance, but it will always be relevant and heart-searching in *every* instance.[15] And the God

[15] For an excellent discussion of the relevance of the Sermon on the Mount to modern life, see Martin Dibelius, *The Sermon on the Mount*, chap. vii.

who in the Sermon lays down these searching requirements is the same God who in the Parables (most clearly
in those of the 15th chapter of Luke) patiently, for-
givingly seeks out those who break His commandments,
to redeem them from destruction. "God makes absolute
moral demands but his love also is infinite. He is a God
of grace as well as of truth." [16] At this point in the
teachings of Jesus, we touch finality and eternity. There
is but one way in which the revelation of God's Will
and God's Love in the Sermon on the Mount and the
Parable of the Lost Sheep has ever been deepened, or is
likely ever to be deepened: by its enactment into deed.
The Cross, where Jesus' enactment of his own teachings
culminated, is more truly eternal than the greatest of his
teachings; but the teachings incomparably illuminate the
meaning of the Cross. Heaven and earth may pass away,
but these Words and this Deed, inseparably associated
each with the other, shall never pass away.

[16] Knox, *op. cit.*, p. 43.

Chapter Two

Jesus as Leader: Then and Now

JESUS was recognized by his contemporaries as a *leader* as soon as he appeared in Galilee, preaching and teaching. There were other preachers and teachers who were mere expositors of Torah, transmitters of tradition, but he was not of that type. He taught "as one having authority, and not as the Scribes." [1] He called disciples to him with the words, "Follow me." [2] Upon a Roman centurion he made the impression of a man under orders, and giving orders, a man born to command — but of superior rank. [3] The authorities both in Galilee and in Jerusalem soon became aware that a movement was afoot under his leadership, and sent deputations to investigate it. Fearing its consequences, they tried to suppress it, like the previous movement led by John the Baptist; [4] but Jesus evaded capture and, to the consternation of his opponents, came to Jerusalem, where he made a disturbing demonstration in the Temple precincts, surrounded and protected by a band of adoring followers.

[1] Matt. 7:29; Mark 1:22.
[2] Matt. 4:19; Mark 1:17.
[3] Matt. 8:5–13; Luke 7:1–10.
[4] See Luke 13:31, 32 for the relations between Jesus and Herod.

It was as one who flatly challenged the authority of his people's existing leaders, demanding their capitulation to the Will of God, against which they had rebelled, that he aroused the delirious enthusiasm of some, during those eventful days in Jerusalem, and the relentless enmity of others. It was as leader of a threatening movement [5] that he was put to death; as a preacher and teacher he might have been left in peace. History records that his death did not stop the movement; it is still going on, and he is still its leader.

I. The dilemma of Jesus' contemporaries: madman or Messiah?

While the contemporaries of Jesus were agreed about the fact that he was a leader, they disagreed violently over the character and quality of his leadership. Fully half of them, to put it bluntly, thought he was crazy. His own family, and perhaps also the Roman procurator — an odd combination — agreed in the view that he was a harmless madman, a religious crank, deserving no worse treatment than to be put under restraint for his own good. His ecclesiastical adversaries, shocked by the revolutionary implications of his attitude toward the Law and the Temple, were inclined to take a more serious view of the case. To them, he was a dangerous fanatic, devil-possessed, who would bring disaster upon the nation if not put out of the way.

[5] On the probable strength of Jesus' movement at the time of his appearance in Jerusalem, see F. C. Grant, *The Gospel of the Kingdom*, pp. 4-11.

Between those who thought him mad and those who took quite an opposite attitude, there seem to have been few defenders of any intermediate position. The boldness of his course did not permit halfway opinions about it. Either one had to doubt his sanity, or one had to cast him for a role of stupendous importance, in some way related to the Hope of Israel and the coming of the Kingdom of God. John the Baptist had already announced the near approach of the Kingdom; Jesus continued the movement founded by his great predecessor, while enormously developing the significance of his message. After John the Baptist's execution, it is reported that there were many (including Herod Antipas himself) who regarded Jesus as John risen from the dead to confound his adversaries and continue his prophetic mission. Others thought he was one of the ancient prophets come back to life, some going so far as to identify him with Elijah, whose return to earth was immediately to precede the coming of the divine Messenger of Judgment.[6] Peter at last (according to the familiar story [7]), in response to a direct question from his Master, blurted out the incredible, the ecstatically joyful surmise that may have been half articulate in the minds of many who had followed Jesus' career up to this point: *"You are the Messiah!"* But no sooner was this confession made than it was met with dark hints of suffering and disaster to come; and the disciples themselves, from this time on,

[6] Mal. 2:17–3:6, and 4:1 ff. On the interpretation of this prophecy current in Jesus' time, see F. C. Grant, *The Gospel of the Kingdom*, pp. 41–44.

[7] Matt. 16:13-20, Mark 8:27-31, Luke 9:18-22.

seem to have grown more and more confused about their Master's leadership. "Messiah, yes, perhaps, but a mad sort of Messiah!" they may have thought.

Madman or Messiah? — that agonizing question must have been tossed back and forth in many minds during the critical days when Jesus made his final challenge to the nation's leaders in the nation's capital. Some who had believed in his Messiahship were dashed down to the opposite conviction by his failure to do what the Messiah was expected to do. (This is one possible explanation of Judas' betrayal.) Others who had believed him a madman were astonished at the words of wisdom that fell from his lips and, unable to doubt his sanity, began to believe in his Messiahship. Jesus himself seems to imply [8] that those who ascribed his work to Beelzebub half recognized that such works could be done only by the power of the Holy Spirit. Such half-hearted opponents must have been in a state of great inward agitation, easily precipitated into ardent discipleship. Sholem Asch has given an unforgettable account, in *The Nazarene*, of the alternating hopes and doubts which must have stirred the populace in Jerusalem from the time the prophet made his entry to the very moment of his death; the wave of popular enthusiasm over the cleansing of the Temple; the disappointment when the prophet failed to defy the Romans as he had defied the Temple priesthood; the confusion and division over his answers to those who had questioned his authority; the consternation when he was delivered into the hands of

[8] Matt. 12:22–32.

the enemy; the hope, even to the last, that God might deliver him by a miracle, when his cup of suffering had been drained to the dregs.

Woe unto us if we had been there! It would take a proud man to be sure of doing the right thing and making the right choice under those perplexing circumstances; and pride would surely have set him on the wrong side, the side of the worldly wise. It was only a few humble and devoted women who followed Jesus to Golgotha and lingered to watch his pitiful end — not because they understood him, but because he had won their love and gratitude. In all that tumultuous city, there was none that understood what he was about, when he set his foot on the *Via Crucis*. If the majority of his Jewish contemporaries rejected him, that was partly because they were Jews, bound in loyal allegiance to the Mosaic covenant and suspicious of any alleged new revelation of God's Will, but it was mostly because they were human! We should probably have done the same. To all human appearances, his promising leadership had ended in a blind alley. Instead of being "the way out," the path he had chosen to take in the crisis of his nation's history would henceforth have to be labeled "Dead End. No Passing Through."

II. How different is our modern situation?

"Blessed are they that have not seen, and yet have believed." Before applying these words of commendation to ourselves, we modern Christians had better consider whether we are not actually in a position to *see more* of the significance of Jesus' leadership and follow him more intelligently, than if we had lived in Jerusalem in his own time, and seen him with our own eyes. We miss many vivid impressions, to be sure, and we are exposed to the danger of conventional lip service toward one whom many generations have been calling "Lord! Lord!" But we have this great advantage, that we can see his way and the way of his rivals in the light of their historic outcome. From our perspective, we can clearly perceive that those who thought Jesus a dangerous fanatic were nearer the truth than those who thought him a harmless crank. Pilate might smile contemptuously at the poor wretch who was called "King of the Jews"; before many centuries had passed this King would show his power by conquering Rome itself. Annas and Caiaphas were nearer the truth than Pilate; but how far from the truth they still were when they judged Jesus' leadership to be purely destructive in its tendency! In point of fact, both the Jewish and the Roman civilizations were headed for destruction under their existing leadership; if it had not been for Jesus' leadership, the soul of these two civilizations might not have been saved for posterity.

Perhaps also we can see from our more distant perspective the necessity for Jesus' puzzling ambiguity in relation to the Messianic hope. It was indeed his mission, we now see, to fulfill the hope of Israel, and make it the common property of mankind; so it was bound to be asserted that he was the Messiah. But had he succumbed to the sort of Messianic expectation that brooded over Jerusalem like a storm about to break — the Zealots' hope of divine assistance in a sudden uprising against Rome — he would have hastened the destruction of his people, and his leadership would have been limited to a particular crisis in his nation's history; whereas his rejection of that limited leadership, and his choice of the way of the Cross, have made him *the Leader* of mankind, for all time. The very behavior which caused all Jerusalem to be offended in him is the securest basis of his absolute claim upon us today. Whether he had thought it all out or whether, as seems more likely, he was led through the deep waters step by step under divine guidance, we can now see that the strange path he took was divinely wise, and the one "way out."

We can now see all this, but is it enough to exempt us from the necessity of faith? Hardly! Historical hindsight is never the equivalent of the practical foresight required in each new historical situation. History never exactly repeats itself if history is really getting anywhere. The fact that Jesus inaugurated a new era in world history has made it necessary for all later generations to make new adventurous decisions for which there is no Scriptural precedent. The fact that Christianity has succeeded in a worldly sense, that it has been accepted as the basis of Western civilization and is at least publicly professed by the nations which have been ruling the globe for the last hundred and fifty years, puts modern Christians in a position unparalleled in the New Testament. Jesus and his followers refused to join the Zealots or to have anything to do with the attempt to correct the injustices of their times by political action; but is this a precedent which should be blindly followed under all circumstances? Should it keep Chinese or Indian Christians today from participating in the rising national-ist movements of their peoples, or Western Christians from endeavoring to defend and reconstruct — by politi-cal means, wherever feasible — the at least semi-Christian civilization which they have inherited from their an-cestors?

It is a travesty upon New Testament Christianity to erect it into an inflexible system of legal precedents and invariable principles. When the New Testament churches faced new issues — as they immediately did — they used the recorded teachings and remembered example of their Lord as invaluable aids to reflection, but their decisions were finally determined by what they believed to be the promptings of his living Spirit. We must do the same. That always takes faith. Faith to believe that Jesus' historic mission to mankind is not yet ended; that he is still "He that cometh" to lead us out of our present dif-ficulties, and we have no need to "look for another." Faith to believe that in spite of all philosophical dif-ficulties living communion with Jesus Christ is really possible for modern men, and he can direct us (if we are willing) as definitely as he did his first disciples. Faith to act, when study and prayer and open-minded dis-cussion have done their best, on what seems to be the true prompting of his Spirit, never quite knowing how it will turn out or whether we may not be mistaken. Faith to try again, after fresh self-examination and fresh reaching out for guidance, as often as we fail, until at last we succeed — or get other marching orders.

With all our historical wisdom, we moderns cannot get beyond the necessity of such faith as this. We must solve our own problems, not by rule and rote, but by listening in faith to that creative Word which breathes through the pages of the New Testament and still struggles for utterance in the modern churches. We have a ground of faith not available to the ancient Church, for we are witnesses to the repeated triumphs of the faith of our predecessors: the faith of our fathers, who built this free Republic as a haven for the oppressed; of the Reformers, who saved European civilization from apparently fatal decay by bringing it back to its Christian sources; of the ancient Latin Church, which saved Roman civilization from barbarism and rebuilt it upon more Christian lines. These are the *gesta Christi*, the deeds of the living Christ through those who have believed on him; and for us they are a powerful incentive, a kind of continuation of the Biblical witness, whereby we are pointed along the path we have to travel. But at every new stage of the journey — above all, when we stand at some great turning point, as we do today — we have to feel our way by faith, trusting that the One whose guidance we are following knows better than we what is around the next bend of the road.

III. False leaders: religious fanatics and political Messiahs

The necessity of faith implies the possibility of doubt, and the legitimacy of discussion. Every generation of

Christians has its own peculiar difficulties about the leadership of Jesus. These should be frankly faced and fully aired, so that when the moment for action comes there may be no inhibitions due to unresolved emotional conflicts, no needless fears that would have been exorcised if they had been honestly confronted. Among the peculiar difficulties of our time I should give first place to the problem of Jesus' relationship to the religious fanatics and political Messiahs who have arisen to plague us in this age. Unless he can be clearly distinguished from both, we are likely to fluctuate in our attitude toward him between delirious enthusiasm and bleak disillusionment, like the Jerusalem populace before the Crucifixion.

Half a century ago, there was no problem about the fanaticism of Jesus. The accepted portrait of "our Lord" was that of a great sage, a paragon of wisdom and virtue according to current modern standards, an esteemed contributor to the sum total of Western culture, an expert in the highest sphere, deserving to have his statue set in the center of that same hall of fame where modern scientists and reformers had more recently been enshrined. If this statement errs by exaggeration, it can nevertheless be concretely illustrated out of such a book as Weinel and Widgery's *Jesus in the Nineteenth Century and After*. The nineteenth century was very sure of its own wisdom. It managed to look up to Jesus as its official leader only by the (to us) transparent device of conceiving him in its own likeness. This tendency is to be seen in so great a book as Seeley's *Ecce Homo*, which with all its profound insight presents Christ, in the last analysis, as having founded, by his new "enthusiasm of humanity," a cosmopolitan moral commonwealth to which modern improvements in communication and modern scientific philanthropy are at last giving the finishing touches. A similar modernistic deformation of the character and teaching of Jesus appears in the work of so learned and accurate a historian as Adolf Harnack, whose *What Is Christianity?* presents what is usually regarded as the classic portrait of the "liberal Jesus."

Doubtless our successors will catch us at the same trick. Even the sincerest desire to follow Jesus can tempt us to project our own hopes and prejudices upon the figure of our Leader. Hence the multiplicity of the Christ-images in Christian iconography, and the bewildering inconsistencies between the various Lives of Christ. But one thing is certain, that no subjective Christ-image can hold our faith, our loyalty, once it is clearly revealed as such; and that is now the case with the nineteenth-century portrait of the liberal Jesus — the genial sage who taught "the higher righteousness and the commandment of love" almost two thousand years before these principles were rediscovered by modern humanitarians. We know now, thanks to Johannes Weiss, Albert Schweitzer, and a host of others who have investigated the eschatological element in the life and teaching of Jesus, that this fiery visionary, who expected to sit on the right hand of Power and come on the clouds of heaven, could never be harmonized with

Victorian society, by any *tour de force* on the part of liberal Protestant apologists. Rather, his relationship to modern Western civilization can be precisely formulated in the proposition that if he is sane, the modern world is crazy; and if the modern world is sane, he is stark mad.

Interestingly enough, the first conclusion drawn from these premises was the latter. The wisdom of this modern scientific age being axiomatic, the visions of Jesus must needs appear against this background as nothing better than the systematic delusions of a paranoiac. Binet-Sanglé, in his book on *La Folie de Jésus* (Paris, 1908), says that in nineteenth-century Europe Jesus would have been put under restraint as a megalomaniac afflicted with mystical hallucinations of a type well known to clinical medicine. Schweitzer himself, who knew Binet-Sanglé's view very well, and grappled with it in his medical studies, adopted an intermediate position. The falsity of all apocalyptic expectations and the validity of modern liberal Christianity were to him also axiomatic; but he clears Jesus of the charge of insanity by tracing his eschatological views to the irresistible influence of the thought-forms of his age; while within the framework of this collective delusion — if the term be not too strong — there was conveyed and preserved for posterity "the eternal religion of love" which was Jesus' real contribution.[9] Both Binet-Sanglé and Schweitzer test the sanity of Jesus by the standards of the modern world.

Now that the self-sufficiency of modern wisdom has

[9] Schweitzer, *Out of My Life and Thought*, pp. 65 ff., 132 ff.

been rudely shaken, many are prepared to turn about and doubt the sanity of the modern world, rather than to doubt the sanity of Jesus. Is it the part of sanity or of madness, they ask, to make men the servants and victims of the machinery they have created; to plow crops under and destroy foodstuffs for the sake of high prices, while there are still starving men on the face of the earth; to keep multitudes of these starving men alive by training them to produce instruments of mutual destruction; . . . and so on *ad nauseam!* The effrontery of it, to call this a sane world and measure the Nazarene by its standards! Why, it is only the small measure of Christianity which Western civilization has taken into its system at certain lucid intervals in its mad history that preserves it from instant and total destruction! Apart from that counter-acting influence, the latent fires of madness burn so fiercely within it that it needs only to get a little crazier at some point — a very, very little crazier — in order to set itself on fire by spontaneous combustion! Before our eyes in recent years one portion of it after another has gone up in crackling sheets of flame like evergreens ignited by a smoldering turf fire. How foolish in such a time to talk patronizingly about "the late-Jewish apocalyptic world-view" as though it were an exploded delusion. It is our modern dream of steady progress through science and invention that has been exploded, instead! [10] "How mortally foolish we mortals are when

[10] I do not mean to suggest that Jewish apocalyptic writings contain no error, and the modern dream of progress no truth. I have already indicated my belief that even in the form held by Jesus and

we are most wise; how divinely wise is Christ when He turns things topsy-turvy."

This mood of humility and self-distrust is favorable for a return from the wisdom of man to the Wisdom of God; but it also facilitates the rise of a new wave of religious fanaticism. When Franklin Roosevelt took office in 1933, in the midst of financial panic and business stagnation, he was able to adopt a very simple policy because of the prevailing mood of despair: "Do something, and if that fails, do something else." Whatever he did, provided only that it was something new and different, was welcomed with thunderous applause. Presently he was surrounded with economic wizards and sociological witch doctors, each with a different nostrum for the ills of the body politic; and while all of them looked sane by comparison with the utter craziness of the existing situation, it was mathematically certain that the great majority of them were cranks and fanatics. If ever a man needed a personal bodyguard of genuine "brain-trusters" it was he! That situation is quite analogous to the existing situation in the religious world. The collapse of human self-confidence and self-reliance in the Western world has opened the way not

---

his disciples (whatever that actually was) ancient apocalyptic hopes need to be interpreted in the light of their actual historic outcome rather than taken at their face value. But everyone who has lived to see this apocalyptic time in which we live must be inclined to mark *up* the percentage of truth in the apocalyptic view of history as *crisis* and *victory-after-disaster*, and mark *down* the percentage of truth in the modern view of history as *cumulative-progress-through-steady-enlightenment*.

only for a return to God and His Anointed One, but also for a stampede towards fanaticism, led by a motley crew of self-anointed Messiahs and self-seeking charlatans. As in every similar age, the true Leader is likely to be lost from view amid the confused swarm of his spurious competitors; and some of our contemporaries who have passed through self-distrust to penitence and new faith are likely to lose their faith again by pinning it on the wrong person.

How are we to distinguish between the true Leader and his pseudoprophetic rivals? It is not easy. It never was easy. It is not as though the name of Christ on the lips of a leader were any guaranty of authenticity; the Christ may at any time "go over to the Gentiles," deserting the temples where men minister in his name but not in his spirit. It is not as though "common sense" were a sufficient criterion; both the true Leader and the fanatic look like fools and madmen when judged by that standard. It is not as though one could dismiss a man as a charlatan when scandal attached itself to his name; that happens to honest men too. Even in the clearest cases of false prophecy it is hard to say just why we are so sure about them. Father Divine's followers say he is God, and wrote the Bible; it is to laugh! And yet we say of Jesus that he is the very power and wisdom of God, whereby the heavens were created and the Scriptures written; and this assertion sounded just as absurd and blasphemous, when first made. I met a man myself in one of the Peace Missions who was regarded as a heretic because although he shouted, "Peace, it's wonderful!" with the best of them, he claimed that Father Divine was not God, but merely the reincarnation of Jesus Christ. I have often chuckled to myself over this odd heresy. And yet by what sort of supernatural certainty am I assured that the revelation in Jesus Christ is once for all complete? If Jesus as the New Moses fulfilled the old Law and inaugurated a New Dispensation, how can we be sure that there are no newer dispensations to come? Our Negro Messiah's followers are ignorant and illiterate, to be sure; but so were the early Christians! Did not Jesus once cry, "I thank Thee, Father, Lord of heaven and earth, that thou hast concealed these things from the wise and learned, and revealed them unto babes!" How do we know that God is not speaking to us out of the mouths of these humble people, as He has done through other despised and rejected groups in the past?

I raise these questions, not because I have any serious doubts on the subject, but to indicate the complexity and subtlety of the issues involved. No wooden yardstick, no mechanical and external criterion can ever settle them, so far as I can see. Our only instrument of precision is a mind and will sensitively alert to the guidance of the Mind of Christ which perpetually mediates the Will of God to the Church, in this and every age. How can we get such a mind and such a will? Not exclusively by mystical exercises. There is a special need, in these wild times, of a group of hard-headed scholars and critical philosophers in the Christian Church, who will maintain a sound tradition in the interpretation of Christian revelation, and relate its higher truth to verifiable truth in every sphere. God cannot contradict Himself; and every alleged new revelation which flies in the face of known facts or flatly contradicts divine laws repeatedly illustrated in the fate of men and nations must be rejected. But while theological experts of this type can do much to protect us against fanaticism, by themselves they are mere Scribes and Pharisees, likely to reject the true Leader along with the false prophets. To offset and supplement their influence, the Church has need of popular preachers, practicing mystics, and simple servants of humanity, who will sense the unique needs of our age as they arise, and apply the Gospel to them convincingly. If theological experts provide a negative defense against fanaticism, these men at their best provide a positive substitute for it; for they sense the same popular yearnings out of which fanatical movements arise, and meet them with honest counsel instead of with deceptive promises. A Church in which neither one of these two groups is lacking will remain true to her Leader and free from fanaticism.

Religious fanatics are not the only will-o'-the-wisps who threaten to lead us astray in this generation; political Messiahs have arisen also, in every quarter of the globe, and the people of the world are if possible more disposed to follow them now than were the Zealots of New Testament times. The Messianic hope is not peculiar to the Jews; it is the expression of a general human craving for more-than-human political leadership in time of crisis, for supernatural help in escaping from woes too burdensome to be borne but from which there seems to be no earthly hope of deliverance. The idea of a God-anointed political Leader is more widespread than we sometimes realize. A Korean student once related in my class an ancient legend current among his people concerning a Leader who was some day to come suddenly out of the foot of a mountain and deliver the land from oppression; whereupon a Slavic student from Central Europe remarked that an exactly similar legend was well known in his country. In times of stress like the present, this universal human longing for divine leadership takes new forms, and fixes itself passionately upon human, all-too-human, objects, to whom it gives the absolute allegiance due only to God or his Anointed One. "Hail, Leader!" it cries, with a salute that is half a prayer. In Europe the formula is *"Long live il Duce! Sieg Heil to the Führer!"* In India men bow their heads and lift their hands in frank adoration of a little man they call *Mahatma.* Even in atheist Russia, the corpse of Lenin and the orders of Stalin are venerated with all the honors which idolators pay to their gods.

We need not go outside our own experience to know what it means to follow a political Messiah. At the close of the First World War, the figure of Woodrow Wilson went up and up in our estimation and expectation, until it took on cosmic dimensions and quasi-divine attributes. Clergymen and laymen alike looked at that portentous sign in the skies with awe, and spoke its human name with bated breath. Truly the Desire of Nations was come, and his name should be called Wonderful, Counselor . . .

Prince of Peace. Then came Versailles . . . and Wood-row Wilson's poor broken human body came down to earth with a thud, like the stick of a spent rocket. That is the fate of all political Messiahs. When a nation is in desperate straits some man of destiny arises, who soars through the very heavens for a time, on the wings of popular expectation; but finally, trying like Icarus to fly too near the sun, he plunges to his doom, carrying down with him the hope and faith of millions. Napoleon, who was such a man, furnished the perfect formula for all his kind when he said, "So long as I am necessary, no power on earth can touch me. So soon as I become unnecessary the stirring of an atom will be sufficient to destroy me."

Christians in our time are under a strong temptation to make over their Leader into the one thing he resolutely refused to be — a political Messiah. The programs of these earthly leaders are so definite, the zeal of their followers is so fervent, the sacrifices they demand are so costly and complete, that they make Christians feel vague, cowardly, and inferior by comparison. Hence the many efforts, in recent years, to offer a "Christian alternative" for these Messianic movements. If this means that Christians must not be less valorous and de-voted, less willing to take definite stands and dangerous risks than their Communist and Nazi contemporaries, this way of taking up the enemy's challenge may be quite fitting and proper for soldiers of the Cross. But if it means that Christians begin to imitate their rivals and make in the name of their Master the same sort of promises that Communists make in the name of Marx, or

Nazis in the name of Hitler, then it involves a fatal betrayal. Jesus, the One Leader of mankind, must not be assimilated to other leaders; and it must be made plain that in every essential respect his leadership differs from that of a political Messiah:

1. *Jesus promises less and achieves more than any political Messiah.* When a man is raised to dizzy eminence upon a great wave of human longing, he is apt to take on the manners of omniscience, and deliver himself of grandiose promises: national self-sufficiency in three easy stages, or Utopia at the end of a five-year plan. Not so the Nazarene. He dashes all the earthly hopes of his disciples, promising them no seats of honor in his Kingdom, but only a share in his cup of bitterness and his baptism of blood. As he enters Jerusalem to challenge his rivals, he is "lowly, and riding upon an ass." Then, after what looks like complete, ignominious defeat on the hill of Golgotha, he slowly gains dominion, century after century, until he rules such a domain as no political leader ever has possessed, and exerts such an influence upon human affairs as no statesman can parallel. Our Napoleons begin by erecting Arches of Triumph and decreeing new laws for a Continent; they end by plunging a whole generation into disillusionment and *mal de siècle*. Jesus begins by setting a cross upon the shoulders of his followers, and ends by crowning them with victory.

2. *Jesus holds his subjects more firmly without coercion than any political Messiah can hold them by coercion.* In times of national emergency, leaders are

elevated at first by pressure from below, but they usually find it necessary to maintain themselves by a great show of power, whereby they impose themselves upon the very people who have elevated them, and carry their followers far beyond their original intention. Jesus, instead of imposing himself upon his followers, gives himself utterly to them, even before they are ready to receive him. He constrains them by gratitude. When they awake to the realization of what he has done for them they find themselves bound indissolubly to him by an unpayable debt, and they are glad to be so bound. Hence his Kingdom holds fast, despite the tenuousness of the bonds that fasten it together, while other kingdoms flame into rebellion and collapse, despite all the precautions of the secret police. As Seeley points out in *Ecce Homo*, most great organizers have said, "I will work my way to supreme power, and then I will execute great plans," whereas Jesus simply announces the advent and the character of his Kingdom — and of this Kingdom founded on generous love, *restraint* of power, divine condescension, there is no end! [11]

3. *For all his gentleness, Jesus makes demands such as no political Messiah would dare to make.* It is easy for political leaders to inspire wholehearted devotion because, as Archbishop Temple once pointed out, they can appeal to both the higher and the lower sides of our hearts at once; the higher side with its willingness to sacrifice for a cause, and the lower side with its pride of race and clan. We are apt to serve Jesus more half-

[11] Seeley, *Ecce Homo*, chap. v, "Christ's Credentials."

heartedly than we serve our political masters, because he refuses to pander to our lower nature, and demands of us a change of heart. We may refuse this demand, and do; but we can never get away from him entirely once we have felt his appeal. Once we have seen his kingdom and his righteousness, we are miserable if we seek anything else first. The only way out of that misery is unconditional surrender to him at the very citadel of our being; we must let him "peg the center" and let everything else arrange itself around him.

If I may be permitted a word of personal witness at this point, it seems to me that the leadership of Jesus is quite incomparable with any other leadership whatsoever. It happens to be part of my professional task to study the lives and teachings of many leaders of religious thought and social action, and to interview many living leaders in person. The leaders to whom I refer are of a far higher type than the religious fanatics and political Messiahs we have just been discussing. To many of them I feel a deep debt of gratitude for the contribution they have made to my own life and thought. But this gratitude does not in any case amount to an unqualified allegiance. It does not lead me to say to any of them, "I am your man. I belong to you, body and soul." Jesus is the only one to whom I am prepared to say that. Plato, Buddha, Francis of Assisi, much as I love and admire them, are still grist for my mill; but I am grist for his mill. I borrow from them, and fit their contributions into my system; but I am glad to be fitted into his system. That is not to say that I would never argue with him about his teachings, or what purport to be his teachings. It would be idolatrous for me to render absolute allegiance to anything in him that is not eternally true; and there is much in his teachings that is temporal and transient. What claims me is not just his teachings, but something to which his teachings and his life, and *the gesta Christi* which his Spirit has worked in later times, all point: his central *meaning* or *intention*, his central *self*, which is one with the Will of God, and makes the Will of God concretely real for me.[12] When I face that central intention, that central self, in him, I am left without any further moral excuse for resisting him, for what he means is God's own eternal Will, which intends my own highest good, and that of all humanity, as we could never realize it for and by ourselves. If, then, there are areas of life where I continue to battle against him, or flee from him, they are areas of sorrow and disaster, and well I know it.

IV. Whither is Jesus now leading us?

Supposing that Jesus should be accepted as the One Leader of mankind in this present chaotic time, where

[12] If it be questioned whether willingness to argue with Jesus over his teachings is consistent with unswerving loyalty to his leadership, I might reply that just such a relationship, on a lower plane, existed between Martin Luther and his devoted follower, Philipp Melanchthon, and exists in our own day between Mahatma Gandhi and Jawaharlal Nehru. (Cf. the frank discussion of Gandhi's opinions and the moving tributes to the power of his personal leadership in Nehru's autobiography, *Toward Freedom*.)

would he lead us? What even now is his intention for us, while we continue to kick against the pricks and try to find the way out by wrong paths? No *detailed* answer to such questions can now be given, for the details of our itinerary emerge only step by step, as we follow the Leader, and our generation has not yet seriously begun to follow him. But a *general* answer can already be given — one which has been expressed repeatedly in recent ecumenical gatherings where Christians have earnestly sought together to learn the Mind of Christ. *It is the intention of our Lord to lead us back to God for judgment, and then, after our minds have been renewed, to lead us forward into a new age, when the foundations of civilization will be freshly laid.*[13]

This need of judgment and renewal applies not only to our secular statesmanship, of whose bankruptcy we are well aware, but to our churchmanship as well. Until recently churchmen were inclined to stand in judgment

[13] Cf. the following words from the *Message to All Peoples*, sent out by the Madras Missionary Conference in 1938: "It is clear that only God can save the peoples, and that the God and Father of our Lord Jesus Christ not only can but will. It must become clearer to us all, however, that the instruments He demands are not men and women of ideals as such, but those who constantly in prayer and worship verify those same ideals before His august will — verify and improve and never cease to re-verify them. . . . Surely God is summoning us in these times to frequent His altars, to learn of Him, and to make His ways known in all the relationships of life . . . bringing the nations and the races and the classes into a community of sympathy for one another, undergirded by a deathless faith in Christ." (Madras Report on *The World Mission of the Churches*, p. 155. Quoted by permission of the International Missionary Council, publishers.)

upon secular civilization and offer themselves complacently as leaders in its reconstruction; now they recognize that they cannot hope to lead the world until they have themselves been led back to God for judgment and renewal.[14] To churchmen first of all, then, Jesus says again in substance what he said to the churchmen of his generation, "Repent, for a new age is at hand into which you cannot enter as you are. . . . Satan has obtained permission to sift all of you as wheat, but I have prayed that your own faith may not fail. And afterward you yourself must turn and strengthen your brothers."[15]

The main purport of Jesus' life and teachings is to be seen in his constant endeavor to point and lead all human institutions, sacred and secular, back to their divine Source, that they may make a fresh start toward their divine Goal. Whether it be the Sabbath, or the Law, or the Temple, or marriage, or property, his queries about every institution are, "What was it made for? What was it originally meant to be, as it issued from the hand of God? How far has it departed from that aim? How will it appear under God's righteous sovereignty, when all its present corruptions are completely purged away?" Such queries he has continually raised, through the mouths of his true prophets and interpreters, in every age. But there come ages like our own, when these

[14] Cf. Madras Report, p. 14: "We see the judgment of God's righteousness upon our society; but we also see His judgment upon our churches."

[15] Cf. Matt. 3:2; Luke 22:31, 32 (adapting his injunction to Peter to the case of his modern disciples).

queries take on a peculiar urgency, because it is plain that institutions as they are cannot go on much longer. Then the problem becomes, "How can we — or at least a small representative group of us — return to God decisively enough, radically enough, so that the power of the future may rest upon us, and our reshaped lives and institutions may be fit to pass through the ordeal of fire which is ahead, and become the nucleus of a new order in the age to come?"

Back to God, forward to a new Christian world order — that is the direction in which our Lord is leading us at the present day. What this means in detail, we must find out as we proceed. It will mean something unique and personal for each one of us, for there is nothing mechanical or uniform about the *imitatio Christi*. It requires different things of each race, each nation, each class, each sex, each individual, which each must discover by experiment. How all these will fit into an organic whole, God knows better than we. All our knowledge and skill, all our intelligence in planning and scheming, all our courage in enduring hardship, will be required. We do not exalt ignorance or impulsiveness into virtues. But at the present moment, at the beginning of the great enterprise of creating a new Christian civilization, our business is to subordinate ourselves, with all our knowledge and abilities, to the One Leader who is appointed to accomplish the whole task. We face the future, therefore, in the mood so graphically suggested by the quotation with which King George VI concluded his Christmas Message for 1939:

I said to a man who stood at the gate of the year, "Give me a light that I may tread safely into the unknown," and he replied, "Go out into the darkness and put your hand into the hand of God. That shall be to you better than a light and safer than a known way." [16]

For us, the hand of God is no unknown hand, but·a warm and human hand, stretched out to us in Jesus Christ for our perpetual guidance. In and through the Man of Nazareth, in and through the living, enlightening Spirit which has been kindled by him in the movement he founded, God has shown forth His eternal Will once for all, and provided leadership for all succeeding generations, relevant to their specific needs and opportunities. To us and to our children's children, we are confident, Jesus will always remain the Prophet of Prophets, God's own Wisdom made powerfully manifest in a human life.

[16] This quotation has been traced to a privately circulated book, *The Desert*, by Miss M. L. Haskins.

Chapter Three

Jesus as Savior: Then and Now

IF some of his contemporaries saw in Jesus the divinely anointed *Leader* of his people, and others only a madman or a charlatan, there were still others — a limited number, then as now — who reacted to him more intimately, and found in him a *personal Savior*.

Many today who recognize the *leadership* of Jesus do not recognize his *saviorhood*. They realize their need of a guiding hand on the long trek through this dark and perplexing world, but that is all. They insist that they are not in need of any medical attention, any radical remaking of their nature, any forgiveness of their iniquities, any supporting strength or grace. They have been once born and once raised, and that is enough. They want no second birth or second childhood, no return from manly independence to childish dependence; they can walk very well, thank you, on their own two feet, when once they have been shown the path. William James has presented an unforgettable portrait of these "once-born" and "healthy-minded" people in his *Varieties of Religious Experience*.

From the point of view of the pastor or priest who

has to give spiritual counsel to individuals, it is of course essential to distinguish between different types of human need. It would be a great mistake to try to cure a really healthy-minded person of morbid obsessions with which he is not plagued, or to try to induce the same kind of conversion in a sedate middle-aged schoolteacher as that which would be necessary to set a carousing drunkard on his feet again. But is it possible to conclude from this that there is no general human need for what may properly be called "salvation"? Is it enough simply to *enlighten* some superior mortals, simply to *show* them the way of life, without bothering them about their sins and weaknesses as one would have to do with less well-bred people?

Whatever uncertainty attaches to these questions in the minds of modern sophisticated Christians, there is no uncertainty about the Biblical answer. The message of the Bible, from start to finish, is a message of salvation addressed to us all on the assumption that we lie under the power of evils from which we cannot deliver ourselves without superhuman aid. While in the Old Testament the promised deliverance may take the relatively external form of escape from Egyptian bondage or restoration from Babylonian exile, it is already suggested by the prophets that bondage and exile are the result of inward bondage to sin and alienation from God. In the New Testament, the Savior who is to bring deliverance from external evils is first of all concerned with the problem of sin. The first chapter of the First Gospel interprets his name, Jesus, to mean that "he

shall save his people from their sins."[1] The Fourth
Gospel describes him as "The Lamb of God that taketh
away the sin of the world."[2] The Epistles of Paul and
John concur in the verdict that we all have sinned, and
need to find in Jesus a Savior to reconcile us to God.[3]
There is much in the reported deeds and words of Jesus
that fits in with this general New Testament description of his role as a savior of sinners. In his own mind,
probably, as well as in that of his followers, a central
part of his mission was "to seek and to save that which
was lost."[4]

I. How Jesus dealt with repentant and unrepentant sinners

The early ministry of Jesus was a mission of healing,
encouragement, and forgiveness among the "lost sheep
of the house of Israel," the so-called "people of the
land," who were regarded as great sinners because they
neither knew nor kept the Law with any care. When
asked why he contaminated himself by eating with
"publicans and sinners," he answered, "They that be
whole need not a physician, but they that are sick. . . .
I am not come to call the righteous, but sinners to
repentance."[5] The irony of this remark is evident in the
light of the parable of the Pharisee and the Publican,
and many other passages. Jesus did not really suppose

[1] Matt. 1:21.
[2] John 1:29.
[3] Rom. 3:23–25; I John 1:7–10.
[4] Luke 19:10.
[5] Matt. 9:12, 13.

that his self-righteous critics were free from unright-eousness, and needed no call to repentance. He regarded them, rather, as too fixed in their rectitude to be capable of salvation: worse sinners than those they looked down upon, because they lacked the humble and contrite heart without which penitence and forgiveness are im-possible. His attitude toward them, when frankly ex-pressed, was one of anger tempered with pity: anger, because they blocked the entrance ways to the Kingdom of Heaven and drove others to despair of God; pity, because they knew not the day of their visitation and chose destruction when salvation was offered them. It surely cannot be claimed that sin, in his eyes, was a disease to which only the dregs of humanity were sub-ject; rather, it was a general state of alienation between man and man, man and God, in which precisely those who supposed themselves to be most free from it and found it hardest to pardon in their neighbors were most hopelessly caught. I cannot believe that his attitude would be different toward those modern Pharisees who claim they do not need to be saved because, try as they may, they cannot see anything wrong with them-selves!

In his dealings with self-confessed sinners, the saving work which Jesus carried on in his lifetime was simple and direct. He dared public disapproval by welcoming them into his society, and even accepting favors at their hands, "while they were yet sinners." In his society, they found their sense of guilt deepened by contrast with his holiness, and their hope of forgiveness quickened by the faith in them he had so convincingly demonstrated. The response, in the case of Mary Magdalene, was given in an act of personal gratitude and adoration; in the case of Zacchaeus, it took the form of an act of restitution which tore up his avarice by the roots. To the woman of evil reputation he then declares, in the presence of her accusers, that "her sins, her many sins, are forgiven," her great love and faith have restored her; while to the crooked tax collector he says, exultantly, "Salvation has come to this house today; Zacchaeus also is a son of Abraham." [6]

So swiftly and unceremoniously does Jesus pronounce the words of absolution over the heads of these notorious sinners, before they have fairly begun their new life, that it may easily appear as though divine forgiveness were an easy thing — a mere gracious wave of the hand, involving no cost and no difficulty. Advocates of the moral or subjective theory of the atonement see in this apparent swiftness and ease the evidence that there is never any impediment to forgiveness on the divine side, but only on the human side — which being overcome by the moral influence of the Savior, the divine absolution comes immediately and automatically. But the cost of salvation in all such cases is actually very heavy, both on the side of the sinner and on the side of the Savior. The sinner is ready for swift and decisive repentance precisely because he has endured so much opprobrium and humiliation that all hope is lost, and he is ready to leap up at the first ray of light that pierces

[6] Luke 7:36–50, 19:1–9.

his darkness. The Savior is able to pronounce absolution immediately because he has entered deeply into the suffering of this soul, shared its sense of desolation, taken its disgrace upon himself publicly, and staked everything upon the prospect of a conversion which, when it occurs, is likely to be absolutely decisive.

How much more costly must forgiveness be, to the Savior and the God he represents, in those far more numerous instances where the sinner does not recognize his guilt, and feels no impulse to make any drastic change in his life! In the course of nature, and under the ordinary course of the Providence of God, the self-righteous sinner (with some aid from long-suffering friends and relatives) pays the costs of his own education. Stiff-necked and unbending in his conscious rectitude, he takes the misfortunes of our common lot indignantly, projecting his guilt upon God and his neighbors, and growing more censorious day by day — until, broken by blows before which a more contrite spirit would only bend, he is ready at last to respond to kindness and mercy when they approach him. Perhaps only then, in the light of an unaccustomed gratitude, will he begin to recognize the error of his ways and see that what he called the injustice of his lot was really the knocking of mercy on his prison door. But this way of inducing repentance is so cruel, so long drawn out, so uncertain of reaching its goal! Surely, the Savior would say to himself, there must be some way of shortening these labor pains and hastening the birth of a soul, if I myself am willing to bear the cost!

II. Divine love and wrath in the Cross of Jesus

It will never be possible fully to enter into the mind of Jesus, nor to imagine what he intended to accomplish by his death. The motives which led him to choose the way of the Cross must have been highly complex, for in this last great decision his whole many-sided life-work came to a head. We have already suggested that, as Leader, Jesus meant to show his people and the world the "way out," when he took this dark way of suffering and sacrifice. In the next chapter we shall see how, by his choice of the Cross, Jesus made a deadly attack upon the massed forces of evil that opposed him. But we are surely within the bounds of probability when we urge that Jesus' Cross was in some way related to that third basic aspect of his mission with which we are concerned in the present chapter: his mission to bring sinners to repentance, and deliver them from the impending wrath of God. Beyond all doubt, he retained to the end that sense of horror at men's guilty alienation from each other, and from God, that urgent passion to bring them reconciliation and forgiveness, to protect them from the coming storm of wrath "as a hen gathers her brood under her wings," [7] which so constantly moved him throughout his ministry. What he sought in life, he sought also in death: to save men from themselves and from the divine judgment which was their due, by identifying himself with them, by taking their sins and sufferings upon himself. In the long hours

[7] Luke 13:34.

when he hung on his Cross, he still sought to mediate divine forgiveness, both to the repentant thief who knew his own need of forgiveness and to the unrepentant persecutors, who "knew not what they did." I am convinced that it was no false "reading-in" when the Apostolic Church saw in Jesus the suffering Servant of the Second Isaiah, who "bare the sin of many, and made intercession for the transgressors"; [8] nor was it mistaken when it found religious peace and acceptance with God ("justification") in his Cross.[9] Jesus *had* actually "died for their sins"; and as our Eternal Contemporary, he died and continues to die for ours.

We are no longer concerned, from this point on, with what the Man of Nazareth *thought* to accomplish by his atoning sacrifice; we are concerned with what he actually *did* accomplish. The distinction is an important one, for at every point what he *was* and *did* outran what he *said* and *thought*. He had his own contemporaries on his mind, and especially that scorned and neglected group known as the "people of the land," the *Am Ha-Aretz*; but the effect of his *deeds* reaches far beyond his little world, to men of every time and place. In and through him, with his eager and passionate consent but beyond his human power to visualize it in its full extent,

---

[8] Isa. 53:12; cf. Isa. 42:1–4, Luke 22:37, 23:34. Prof. Bowman of Western Seminary, Pittsburgh, suggests that the voice which Jesus heard at his baptism (Mark 1:11) called and ordained him specifically to be God's Suffering Servant (cf. the echo of Isa. 42:1 in Mark 1:11) and he consciously began his ministry with the intention of carrying out this mission. See Bowman's forthcoming book on *The Intention of Jesus*.

[9] Rom. 5:8–11.

God worked a work of reconciliation that brought all men, potentially, into fraternal fellowship with one another and filial fellowship with their Creator.

God worked this work; let that be clear at the start. Let it never be suggested for a moment that a merciful Christ died to propitiate an angry God, grasping the sword of divine justice with bleeding hands, midway in its swing.[10] Let it never again be said that wrath is deeper than mercy, justice more basic than love in the divine nature. Luther was right: "Love is God's own proper work; wrath His alien work." [11] It is on account of confusion and moral revulsion at this point that all "penal satisfaction" theories of the atonement have fallen into disrepute. Yet they were not wrong in their insistence that the wrath of God, however secondary it may be, is frightfully real, and cannot be set aside without tragic suffering. The God of love takes this suffering upon Himself through the Savior who represents Him; while the Savior in turn participates in the wrath of the God who sends him. He is a man of wrath, as truly as God is a God of wrath. The same lips which voice his gracious love to those who receive him convey his condemnation to those who reject him. Their fate goes through his heart, and he suffers tortures on their behalf, but so long as they oppose him, he opposes them, and his anger blazes out hotly against them: "Ye serpents,

[10] There are many examples of this conception in Christian art as well as in theology. Two especially significant paintings are in the Klosterkirche at Heilsbronn in Bavaria, where Christ appears grasping the sword of justice wielded by God the Father.
[11] Quoted in Sydney Cave's *Doctrine of the Work of Christ*, p. 181.

ye generation of vipers, how can ye escape the damnation of hell?" [12]

What is the wrath of God? It is no imaginary bogey to scare children, but a reality with which every statesman needs to reckon. It is the necessary opposition which develops between God and His creatures whenever they try to live as though He did not exist, or as though some other will than His were finally authoritative. When any creature thus turns against his Creator, however gaily and unconsciously, however unselfish and idealistic the aims which are put in place of the divine Will, the result is disastrous, and God Himself with all His infinite love and might cannot make it otherwise.

As my Creator and Sustainer, God must renew my life constantly from His everlasting springs; so soon as I turn against Him and cut myself off from my Source, the very life that animates me begins to fail and droop toward death. As the Orderer and Governor of all He has made, God lays down in the structure of the world and the structure of my soul the lines along which I must proceed if I am to find my highest good; when I deviate from those lines He must oppose me, for my own good as well as the good of the world at large. Above all, when I become a member of some self-assertive group that pursues its own interest with reckless disregard for the general good, setting itself up as a rival sovereignty in the divine domain, then how can God do other than to oppose me until I sever my connection with the rebels and cross over to make my surrender?

[12] Matt. 23:33.

There is nothing capricious nor tyrannical in all this; God *must* assert His authority over me if He is to do me good, for He is the very Source of my being and well-being, "from whom all blessings flow." Were He to permit me without any form of opposition to abandon Him for another sovereign, He would be showing indifference to the fate of His creature and child; for it is plain that any other sovereignty than His is sure to collapse ultimately, bringing disaster to all its adherents.

Despite the silence and the invisibility of God, despite His "slowness to anger," despite His long tolerance of evil men and evil institutions, we human beings have always been uneasy in our religious conscience, vaguely conscious that we deserve God's wrath. We feel sinful, guilty, afraid in the sight of God, not merely because of specific acts which we know to be evil, but because, as Professor Wieman suggests, we have a feeling that "what we do is against God even when we do not know specifically what it is that is wrong." [13] Something has got between us and God — something which we are responsible for, but which we do not know how to set aside; and because of this cleavage, this blockage on our side, "God gives and we are unable to receive."[14] The sense of original sin springs from a vague awareness of this collective and chronic alienation of mankind from its divine Source. It is our subjective human response to the objective overshadowing of life by the divine wrath.

[13] *Christian Century*, Jan. 25, 1939, p. 117.
[14] *Ibid*.

Strange and pathetic are the devices by which men have sought to assuage their sense of guilt and gain acceptance with God. The principle behind them all was clearly stated to me once by an Irish Catholic layman who was explaining why he had lately gone off on a week's retreat and performed many difficult and irksome spiritual exercises. "I felt," he said, "as if I hadn't been living or praying as well as I ought, and I wanted to make it up to God by doing something hard." [15] That is the simplest and best explanation that could be given to account for all the fastings, vigils, flagellations, pilgrimages, and other forms of self-mortification that abound in medieval Christianity. It is also the best explanation of the ancient institution of blood sacrifice. It represents an attempt to do something hard and costly, something that hurts and punishes, to "make it up to God." Whether it is only the firstlings of the flocks and herds that are offered up, or whether in time of grave distress it is actually one's own first-born who is offered up, the motive in either case is not merely to beg or persuade by giving costly gifts, but also, I am sure, to make atonement for sin by doing something hard. The

[15] President A. C. McGiffert, Jr., of the Pacific School of Religion, discussing this illustration with me, remarked that he thought an even better illustration of the nature of the general human guilt-feeling was to be found in the fact that, at a certain county fair, a machine for kicking yourself was enormously popular. People are actually willing to pay for the privilege of giving themselves "a swift kick well placed." They not only enjoy doing "hard things," they enjoy doing painful and self-tormenting things that give unconscious relief to their unconscious conviction that they deserve to be thrashed. I accept this illustration as a humorous intensification of the idea I am trying to convey.

unspoken query behind the institution of blood sacrifice, in every part of the world, is the pathetic query put to the Lord by Micah:

> Wherewith shall I come before the Lord, and bow myself before the high God? Shall I come before him with burnt offerings, with calves a year old? Will the Lord be pleased with thousands of rams, or with ten thousands of rivers of oil? Shall I give my first-born for my transgression, the fruit of my body for the sin of my soul? [16]

The Lord's answer to Micah, simple and joyful as it sounds by contrast, was not destined to give the human spirit any permanent relief from its sense of alienation. "To do justly and to love mercy and to walk humbly with thy God" — these are clear and simple requirements, compared with the elaborate sacrificial rituals they tended to replace, but they are infinitely difficult to fulfill. What a terrible thing it is after all to be told, "I will have mercy and not sacrifice," [17] or to be reminded of the great words of the Psalmist: "The sacrifices of God are a broken spirit: a broken and a contrite heart, O God, thou wilt not despise." [18] The requirement of true justice and unfeigned mercy was so hard for Judaism to fulfill that there was an irresistible temptation to replace these "weightier matters of the law" with a multitude of little detailed requirements — "mint, anise, and cummin" — which could be definitely complied with. The requirement of real humble contrition in the

[16] Mic. 6:6, 7.
[17] Hos. 6:6; Matt. 9:13.
[18] Ps. 51:17.

sight of God was so hard for medieval Catholicism to fulfill that for the sake of poor human nature it had to be softened down: Let a dash of the fear of hell, technically known as "attrition," be mixed with as many little "good works" as could be heaped together, and let the remaining deficiency be made up with unlimited paternosters and plenteous drafts upon the treasury of the merits of the saints; the result would not quite be equal to one genuine act of contrition, but it might perhaps serve to get one a low passing grade in the Great Examination! Whether popular Protestantism has done better, others can judge better than we. One fears that the "faith" which Protestantism has put in place of Jewish and Catholic "works of the law" has itself in many cases become the means of a new evasion of reality, a new set of surrogates (this time in the form of correct doctrinal beliefs) replacing the genuine act of self-surrender which is required.

How can we do what the Lord requires of us? How can we be just enough, merciful enough, contrite enough, to feel right when we stand in God's presence? How can we escape from the entanglement of sin and avert the divine wrath? The answer surely is that we cannot, unless God enable us; and God himself cannot enable us so long as we are trying to be "just with God" by our own unaided powers. This is a desperate truth which apart from the full, unadulterated faith of Evangelical Christianity is fit only to drive us to atheism, profligacy, or suicide; but in the mouth of a Paul, a Luther, a Bunyan, a Wesley it is the necessary preface to salvation, the "wicket-gate" leading to the foot of the Cross, where the burden of sin will drop from our shoulders and leave us at last free to live with all our powers. For if the message of all these great Evangelicals is true, God has "made it up" for us by doing "something hard," "something costly." He has done for us in advance, through Christ, what we could never do for ourselves if we slew sacrificial beasts and piled up meritorious deeds till the end of time. He has performed a Sacrifice to end all "sacrifices," a Good Work to end all "good works." He has come and stood in our place, under the shadow of our guilt and His own wrath, so deeply identified with our lot that — if we are willing — a mystic sharing can now take place between us, whereby His infinite goodness passes over to us, while the weight of our guilt and terror passes over to His strong shoulders. The enmity between us is slain by the same cruel hammer blows, the same inhuman mockery, the same utter humiliation and desolation of spirit which tortured and killed the Man of Nazareth upon his Cross. The grief of Jesus at our sins, his bearing of the sense of estrangement and guilt which is properly ours, offered up to God that full contrition and full obedience to His Will which were needed to permit the divine love to break through the involuntary barrier of the divine wrath; and a unity between God and man was thus established which was only faintly foreshadowed before, and can never again be wholly destroyed. Henceforth, it is every man's heritage, whether he knows it or not, to be a son of God. His sonship is bought and paid for, at infinite cost; he has only to claim it and enter into it. God has "made it up" with man, through Jesus, and through him also man has "made it up" with God.

Perhaps it may help to make our meaning clearer, at this most crucial point, if we ask how the relationship of man and God differed, before and after Calvary. In one sense this is a misleading question, because the drama of reconciliation is not just a series of dated events — Creation and Fall, *circa* 4004 B.C., according to Ussher's chronology, Redemption *circa* A.D. 30 — but a drama that must be repeated in the history of each individual human being, if he is really to "get right with God." God suffers specific pangs for each of us, not merely one crucifixion for all of us. Yet in another sense it must be said that the event of Calvary makes all the difference in the world.

How? *Not* that God was unforgiving before and forgiving afterward; the Lamb was slain on God's eternal altar "before the foundation of the world." *Not* that God was both wrathful and loving before and only loving afterward; God's wrath is still poured out, and will forever be poured out, upon those who do not meet the conditions of entrance into His favor. But in and through the crucifixion of Christ God has performed a hard and costly Deed which makes His love newly accessible, and makes the world permanently different for those who, coming within the radius of influence of the Deed, respond to it affirmatively. God in Christ has made saving, sacrificial *contact* with the world's burden of iniquity: while continuing to repel and oppose it by His holiness, and expose its "exceeding sinfulness" by the ghastly horrors it inflicts upon His Holy One, He has taken its suffering and its guilt upon Himself, and borne for us what we cannot bear of ourselves — the awful weight of guilt which alienates us from Him, from our neighbors, and finally even from ourselves.

Had this Deed never been done at any time in history, the Lamb slain in eternity would be cold comfort to us. Or rather, we can believe in the eternal Lamb only because on Calvary, in the days of Pontius Pilate, God's sacrificial love actually got into history, where it could reach us. In and through this willing human Servant, God did what could only be done through a historic Son of Man: brought His everlasting mercy into appealing personal *touch* with men in their actual condition — most especially with those who directly felt the reverberations of this great sacrificial Deed. Through Jesus' death for our sins there was established a *historic nucleus of right relationship between God and man* — a relationship of faith, in which man does the right as God gives him to see the right, trusting God for "grace to cover all his sin" — and membership in this nucleus is open to all, righteous or wicked, who are willing to be received into that kind of relationship. That is the difference that Calvary made, as I see it. Words are inadequate to describe it, but of one thing I am morally certain, that it was something objectively *done and accomplished*, not merely a new "manifestation" of what was already just as true before Jesus died.

I know of course that this whole idea of an objective atonement, a finished work, a great transaction, which was so precious to our Puritan forefathers and so basic in all the evangelistic preaching of the last century, has now come to seem hollow and unreal. All the theological apparatus that used to be connected with it — imputed sin and imputed righteousness, penal suffering and vicarious sacrifice — has now been relegated to our museums of colonial antiquities, along with the spinning wheel and the warming pan. I have no sentimental interest in this old-fashioned mental furniture; let it continue to gather dust and quaintness in innocuous desuetude (as Grover Cleveland would say) if its work is really over, and its function superseded by more modern styles of thought. But I am disturbed with a recurrent suspicion that, far from being superseded, it has simply been put aside without anything to take its place. If the objective atonement was only a legal fiction, invented by theologians, this might be good riddance; but if, as we have contended, the wrath of God and the alienation of man are tragic realities, then it is the height of folly to refuse to grapple with them. The effect of ignoring them — of acting as though we were fit to bear the weight of guilt which only God can bear — is only to drive them inward from our conscious to our unconscious mind, whence they work out again to plague us in various guises.

The modern man's consciousness — or rather *unconsciousness* — of sin and guilt is a weird and amazing phenomenon. Reacting against what he is pleased to call the "morbidness" of his ancestors, he has adopted a resolutely cheerful and commendatory attitude toward himself, restricting his admitted lapses to a short manageable list of minor faults, and refusing to admit that there is anything generally or fundamentally wrong with him. Actually, the whole main drift of modern life, with its persistently man-centered, self-sufficient attitude, is one huge affront to God; and the sense of guilt arising from participation in this manner of life is too powerful to be laughed off or blandly dismissed. What happens to it has been very well described by Dean Lewis J. Sherrill,[19] whose findings are based upon a wealth of pastoral and clinical observation. Where the individual carries about with him "a deep guilt-feeling which he is unwilling to face," he is likely to give "excessive attention to some relatively unimportant sin." This minor sin, through carrying too heavy a burden of concern, may become the nucleus of a neurosis or psychosis, in which the repressed guilt-feelings burst forth with morbidly concentrated intensity. Or if this minor sin be cured, the feeling of forgiveness may be experienced in such "richness" that the individual becomes "incapable of seeing the more malignant remaining elements in himself," like the heroine of Rachel Crothers' *Susan and God*. Meanwhile these "malignant elements" go on producing their inevitable psychological

[19] "The Sense of Sin in Present-Day Experience," *Religion in Life*, autumn, 1939, pp. 504–15.

effects; but since they are not recognized as sinful, the sinner feels anxiety, depression, suicidal impulses, or hatred of his fellows, instead of guilt.

Not only the prevalence of mental disease in recent years, but that of war and race hatred as well, is intimately related to this situation. Refusing to recognize his guilt, modern man sometimes drives it inward till it wrecks his mind, but more often he projects it outward till it wrecks his social order. The Allied Powers lay the whole burden of their war guilt upon the Germans; the Nazis respond by laying their guilt upon the Jews and the English; the rest of humanity now finds in Hitler the perfect scapegoat that taketh away the sin of the world. Can humanity possibly be saved from hell upon hell — each one opening into another and darker one — unless it becomes conscious of its guilt as the root of all its ills, and seeks *forgiveness* of God and man as the first and most essential step in its salvation? Who would be prepared to estimate all the political and social consequences if a nation should some day perform a sincere act of public repentance of its sins and genuine forgiveness of its enemies; or failing that, if some group within the nation should perform a dramatic and effective act of confession and atonement on behalf of the nation![20]

[20] I mean this very seriously. I was in Germany in 1921–22 and know at first hand the terrible effect of the "war guilt" clause upon German mentality. It is unlikely that the U. S. A. or any other nation will ever publicly confess its guilt for the present world conflict; but if churchmen, perceiving their country's guilt more clearly than their compatriots, will publicly declare and confess their country's share

III. How "the grace of the Lord Jesus Christ" saves modern sinners

But if atonement has been offered once for all upon the Cross, why should any further acts of atonement be necessary? So to speak is to miss the whole meaning of the work of Christ. He comes to us as the Mediator of God's forgiving love, breaking a way through our despair or our pride and bringing us actually back into living union with God's will. Now either this does not truly occur at all, or, if it occurs, it requires and constrains us to forgive others as we have been forgiven, to atone for the sins of others as Christ has atoned for ours, to bear our cross for others as he has borne his for us, to mediate his love to others as he has mediated God's love to us. This necessity of passing on forgiveness and atonement is most explicitly stated in the teaching of Jesus and in the witness of his apostles. "If ye forgive men their trespasses, your heavenly Father will also forgive you; but if ye forgive not men their trespasses, neither will your Father forgive your trespasses." [21] "He laid down his life for us, and we ought to lay down our lives for the brethren." [22] Either, then,

---

in causing this war — for instance, by such acts as high protective tariffs and Oriental exclusion laws — it will do much to clear the air for the coming Peace Conference. *Never again must a peace treaty have such a war guilt clause as that in the Treaty of Versailles.* Might not the next treaty even begin with a clause acknowledging *general community in guilt,* and *common need of a new and better order?* Churchmen should urge this, insistently.

[21] Matt. 6:14, 15; compare the parable of the debtor, Matt. 18:23–35.
[22] I John 3:16.

a person has genuinely entered through Christ's mercy into God's own disposition, and despite all remaining sins is willing to suffer much for people who have no "claim" on him — including strangers, enemies, and outcasts — doing good to them and bearing evil from them without personal resentment; or else, for him, Christ has died in vain and he is still under God's wrath. All who are truly saved by Christ's atoning sacrifice are helping him bear his Cross, making up for the sins of others, forgiving and saving others in his name. If they have none of his forgiving disposition, they have none of his forgiveness; if they are not in some sense cosaviors and cosufferers with him, we may know that they have not received his salvation and are yet in their sins — yes, even if they be upright citizens, prelates of the Church, or chief workers in the Ladies' Aid! Ability to "love much" [23] without hope of recompense, inability to cherish a grudge, are perhaps the only essential requirements of a Christian; but they are requirements that cut deep, and have far-reaching consequences.

The most important of these consequences is what the Protestant Reformers used to call the "priesthood of all believers." Christ's priestly work of bringing divine forgiveness to overburdened consciences and peace to despairing souls is a work which he delegates not only to the official clergy of his Church, but to every individual Christian. It is good that there should be trained father-confessors to pronounce priestly absolution in

[23] Luke 7:47, "She loved much: but to whom little is forgiven the same loveth little."

the name of Christ and the Church; but there are many laymen who do the thing very effectively, simply by receiving wrongdoers into fellowship and declaring God's mercy to them — as much by attitude as by speech. The truest act of priestly absolution of which I have any personal knowledge was performed by a nurse in a hospital. They brought in from the ambulance a young woman who had been stabbed in a drunken brawl in a disreputable quarter of the city. It was seen at once, upon examination, that the case was perfectly hopeless, and the nurse was asked simply to sit by the unconscious girl until death came. As she sat looking down, thinking what a pity it was that a face as young as that should have such coarse lines upon it, the girl opened her eyes. "I want you to tell me something, and tell me straight," she said. "Do you think God cares about people like me? Do you think He could forgive anyone as bad as me?" The nurse (so she told me, in recounting the incident) didn't dare to answer at first — not until she had reached out to God for a kind of authorization, and reached out toward the poor girl, till she felt one with her. Then she said, knowing now that it was true, "I'm telling you straight: God cares about you, and He forgives you." The girl gave a little sigh, and slipped back into unconsciousness, the lines on her face changing as death approached. I believe that something momentous happened between God and that girl through that nurse, and that it had something to do with what happened long ago on a certain "green hill far away outside a city wall." That is to say, it was through Christ, in his name and spirit, that the nurse pronounced those words of absolution. Apart from Christ, neither the girl's question nor the nurse's answer would ever have been spoken.

If Christ still operates in our midst, through his true followers, to bring pardon to repentant Magdalenes, he also operates in our midst to make costly atonement for self-willed and tough-minded sinners, doing them good in advance of their repentance, at the risk of failure and scorn. A striking instance of such costly action was related to me by a Chinese pastor in a port city of the Far East. As a young man, he was in business in Java, and very successful. One of his competitors adopted "cutthroat" methods which put him in a serious dilemma: either to descend to similar methods, or be gradually driven to the wall. He felt that as a Christian he could not possibly do what his competitor was doing; so, being sole owner of his business, he made an appraisal of its value, wrote out a check for the whole amount, and handed it to his competitor, saying that he much preferred to give him the business rather than have relations between them go on as they were going. The result was startling, but not what he intended. "I meant," said the pastor, "to gain my brother, and make my enemy into my friend in Christ; but he only felt humiliated at his loss of face, and committed suicide." Despite this tragic outcome, which may have been due to lack of tact or traces of self-righteousness in the young Christian's manner, or again may not have been due to any failure on his part, I still feel that this is a clear illustration of the effect of a sacrificial deed upon the sort of man who would not have been moved by any amount of pious talk, or by any deed less costly. Suicide and radical conversion are sometimes only a hairsbreadth apart. The suicide of Judas, as well as the repentant tears of Peter, proves that atoning good will like Christ's is "a *power*, not a platitude."

The Church of Christ is the main channel through which such creative good will flows down through the centuries. She has no more important function than to re-enact the Cross in relation to all sorts of specific situations. All that she teaches about the life of her Master, all that she proclaims about the nature and will of God, all the sacramental grace that she dispenses in her solemn ceremonies, all properly issue in action that meets particular evils with appropriate deeds of atonement. Unless her other activities do issue in such morally creative deeds, they are vain. But when the Church falls into vain, self-centered ecclesiasticism, as she sometimes does, that does not stop the operation of Christ's saving work in the modern world. Christ is not only the Head of the Church, he is the Head of Humanity as well; and his Spirit operates through other than ecclesiastical channels.

Borthwick, in his painting "The Presence," presents a problem which all high churchmen must lay seriously to heart: Where is the "Real Presence" of Christ most fully operative? Down there by the high altar of the cathedral, where the priest elevates the wafer and the faithful bow in worship, or back here near the main entrance, where an invisible Comforter looks with compassion upon a distraught woman kneeling in despair? There are many moderns who, like this woman, find ecclesiastical Christianity too technical, too formal, too unreal to attract them to its high altar; but Christ nevertheless moves in their midst. Abraham Lincoln was too troubled by the clamor of the sects, too perplexed all his life with unresolvable difficulties to find himself fully at home in any church; [24] but who can doubt that Christ was with him, not only to sustain him in his dark hours, but through him to sustain multitudes of others? No priest ever dispensed the grace of the Lord Jesus Christ more richly from a silver chalice than Lincoln by his compassion upon cowards and traitors; no preacher ever proclaimed the Gospel more clearly than when, in answer to a woman who complained that he ought to be more eager to destroy his enemies, he answered, "Do I not destroy them when I make them my friends?"

Through multitudinous channels, ecclesiastical and nonecclesiastical, the veritable "grace of the Lord Jesus Christ," the same shed forth on Calvary, is flowing about us in this contemporary age; and since no one can truly be touched by it who is not impelled to pass it on, it will continue to flow through human life forever, as long as there is life on this planet. That is surely a large part of the truth in the idea of Christ's perpetual presence with us, as our Savior from sin; but it is not the

[24] It is true that Lincoln drew closer to the Church in the last critical years of his life, and often went privately to prayer meeting in a certain Washington church; but his Christianity was, to the end, of an unconventional pattern, which opposed conscientious scruples to church membership.

whole truth. Christ is not merely the distant spring from which the stream of mercy that flows by my door first started, long ago; it may also be said of his mercy that it "droppeth as the gentle rain from heaven." The whole climate of earth, the whole relationship between earth and heaven, is different since he came. Except for those who ignorantly or stubbornly persist in living as though it were still Before Christ, the whirlwind of the divine wrath no longer terrifies, the mercy of God descends like gentle rain upon His redeemed people; and the name of God, when He thus effectively breaks through His wrath, slays the enmity, and descends to bless us, is forever and inevitably synonymous with the name of Jesus. Jesus acts upon us mediately through those whom he has touched, but he also acts upon us more immediately, as God's own wisdom and power, which first found effective union with and entrance into human life in the Man of Nazareth. In both senses, he is our Eternal Contemporary.

We know of course that the salvation which Jesus has brought us did not absolutely begin with him, *nor is it yet complete*. Who needs to be reminded of that, in these days of world catastrophe! It was his divine mission not only to save a few individuals from their sins, but to save the world generally and collectively. He has not yet done it, except in parts and portions. We shall have to consider the unfinished portion of his task, and what he is doing about it, in our next chapter. But this much he has already accomplished: he has established peace between God and great multitudes of his erring and alienated children, and sent them forth, as he sent forth the twelve, "as sheep in the midst of wolves," to give Christ's peace to others as he has given God's peace to them. It is a troubled peace, for they cannot be content to keep it to themselves, and when they try to spread it they have to contend with "fightings and fears"; but until this inner center of peace is established, all hope of world peace in the external sense is surely vain. The beginning of all good is forgiveness and reconciliation, as the beginning of evil was sin and alienation.[25]

To those who have known what it is to be at peace with God and their own souls, and spread that great peace to others, salvation is already an accomplished fact. They know the meaning of "eternal life in the midst of

[25] Karl Heim uses the following figure to show the *primacy* of the problem of sin and forgiveness: In a great factory run by electricity, the machinery has come to a stop. Workmen examine the machinery itself, and the transmission system; nothing wrong. For so general a disorder, there must be a very central cause! At last the central cause is found: the fuses in the basement have all been blown out. Until *connection with the source of power* has been re-established through the replacement of the fuses, it is futile to tinker with the machinery. So sin reduces all human effort to futility, by breaking or impairing the connection between us and our divine Source. The restoration of that connection is necessarily the *first* step in our salvation. We may add that divine forgiveness is our *last* need as well as our *first*; for human life, even among the saints of God, is never finally and completely redeemed from all shadow of sin, all sense of failure. At the end, we must all give an unfinished lifework back into the hands of God, praying that He may forgive its dropped stitches and finish it for us. God's forgiveness both gives us power to do good works and enables us to bear the failures and sad lapses which mar even the best of human works.

time, by the strength and under the eyes of God." While they contend with evil, and strive to extend the area within which God's forgiving love effectively operates, they have an inner contentment and an inner source of strength which are enough, amply enough, to uphold them against the worst that the world can do to them. So though the Kingdom of God goes glimmering over the horizon, and the hosts of darkness swarm out and seize the sovereignty of earth again and again, faith still can sing,

Salvation *is created* in midst of all the earth!
Alleluia!

Chapter Four

Jesus as Victor: Then and Now

THE life of Jesus was not only the life of a *leader* — the great trail-blazer who showed mankind the way out of the woods. It was not only the life of a *savior* — the Suffering Servant, "bruised for our iniquities," who through his sacrifice restored us to a new life of fellowship with God. It was also a life of incessant *conflict* and *combat*, waged on our behalf against the forces of evil that have enslaved us, and ending in a decisive *victory* over them.

Whether we consider him from the point of view of his apparent intentions or from the point of view of his actual accomplishments, Jesus was a great fighter, a great strategist, a great conquerer. If he had written his memoirs, they might have been entitled *Mein Kampf* ("my battle"). He was not content to show a way of escape from the evils of this world, or to rescue some little company of souls from the clutches of an Adversary too strong to overthrow; he made a frontal attack upon the forces of evil, seeking out their very center with great strategic skill; and though he fell in the attack, he brought about their defeat and broke their power. To his followers he left the task of "mopping up," the task of repeatedly putting down the desperate uprisings of a shattered army which refuses to admit defeat but is powerless to regain the commanding position it once held. The results of the great victory he won are still incompletely consolidated, and may remain uncertain till the end of history; but in principle it was a complete *victory over the world*, which guarantees that in the end as in the beginning it is God's world, and not the devil's.

I. Jesus' victorious battle with "The Prince of This World"

Whatever may be our own view of the nature of evil, there can be no doubt that Jesus viewed it very realistically, as an insurgent power that had built up a rival government on God's earth, and transformed it into a demon-ruled domain. An Adversary is at work in the world, who has sowed tares among the wheat and raised up for himself a liberal crop of followers.[1] The sicknesses and other troubles with which the children of earth are afflicted are not simply part of God's good providence, which they must humbly accept; these evils are largely the work of the Adversary, and contrary to God's will. The mental tortures which men endure are not merely the effect of their sins — though they may be connected with them — but to a large extent they are due to demon possession, to the malicious assaults of the Evil One.[2]

[1] Matt. 13:38, 39.
[2] Mark 1:23-27, and many other passages.

When Jesus retired to the desert to think out his mission it seemed to him that the Adversary assailed his mind, and tried to confuse his thinking; but he, eluding these assaults and avoiding all plans of action that would compromise his position, set himself deliberately to break the power of the Usurper, and restore the Kingdom of Earth to its rightful heavenly Ruler. His early ministry was full of works of healing; they were works of compassion, but at the same time acts of war: compassion upon the poor human victims, war upon their demonic oppressors. One of the most jubilant moments in his life came when some of his followers, who had been sent out to announce the coming of God's Kingdom in all the towns and villages of Israel, returned and reported that evil spirits obeyed them when they invoked his name.

"Lord," they said, "the very demons obey us in your name." He said to them, "Yes, I watched Satan fall from heaven like a flash of lightning. I have indeed given you the power of *treading on serpents* and scorpions and of trampling down all the power of the Enemy; nothing shall injure you." [3]

It might not be far from the truth to suggest that in Jesus' eyes this first success of his disciples was like the opening skirmish in a great war. It was like the first clashes between Judas Maccabeus' insurgents and the

[3] Luke 10:17–19. (From *The Bible, a New Translation*, by James Moffatt. Harper & Brothers, Publishers.) The mission of the "seventy" in Luke is apparently identical with the mission of the twelve in Matt. 10.

troops of the Seleucid ruler, or like the skirmishing at Lexington and Concord in the American Revolution. In itself it was of slight importance, but it proved that his raw troops were able to do battle successfully on God's behalf against the "Prince of Darkness," without trembling or running away; and he was therefore encouraged to lead them up against the stronghold of rebellious Israel, in Jerusalem, to risk all in a decisive battle against the dark forces that had gained such power over God's people in that "evil and adulterous generation." His wrestling was not with flesh and blood, and his weapons were not made with hands; but it was a real military campaign that he was waging, in spirit and intent.

Why did Jesus identify the power of the Adversary with Israel — God's chosen people — *instead of with the tyranny of pagan Rome?* We cannot know what passed through his mind, but a glance at the historical situation may enable us to discern some of the reasons for what looked to his contemporaries like a singularly unpatriotic judgment.[4]

---

[4] New Testament critics will doubtless shake their heads over the following paragraphs, because they give a "psychologizing treatment" of Jesus' motives. It is customary to say now that no "biography" of Jesus can be written, because neither the sequence of events in his career nor the motivation of his actions can be securely established. Let us agree that all connected accounts of his lifework must use subjective interpretations to some extent. But New Testament scholars have no right to forbid the use of such interpretations (frankly recognized for what they are), for that would be to forbid the preaching of the Gospel! *The Gospel is a story, and the story must be told*, with the aid of conjecture when necessary. The most dramatic events in all history must be treated dramatically, and that means some sort

Once before in the recent past Israel had been unbearably oppressed by foreign tyranny, under Antiochus Epiphanes, last of the Greek Seleucids to rule over Palestine. Antiochus desecrated the Jewish Temple, setting up an idol ("the abomination of desolation," as the Book of Daniel calls it) in the Holy of Holies, and tried both by violence and by diplomacy to Hellenize and paganize the Jews. A successful revolt under Mattathias and Judas Maccabeus led to the recapture and rededication of the Temple in 165 B.C. and the inauguration of an independent Jewish state under their successors, the Hasmonaean princes.

But this miraculous deliverance from foreign tyranny led to a great disillusionment. Both as guardians of the public welfare and as guardians of religious institutions, the Hasmonaeans turned out to be a degenerate line, and eventually (in a dynastic quarrel) betrayed the country their fathers had rescued from the Greeks into the hands of the Romans. Under the Hasmonaeans and under the Idumaean puppet-kings who succeeded them, the political and religious leadership of Palestine became almost unbelievably corrupt. In Jesus' lifetime there were men of indubitable integrity in high social position, especially amongst the Scribes and Pharisees; but the men at the top — who had to deal with the Roman

---

of "psychologizing treatment." Critics have a right to object to any motives being ascribed to Jesus which are out of character or anachronistic; but there is no real anachronism in trying to feel one's way into his motives by means of analogies drawn from earlier or later history, if only the established character of Jesus and the special conditions of his time be clearly kept in mind.

procurators in Jerusalem or the local puppet-kings elsewhere — were a worldly, cynical, time-serving lot. Though they might hold high religious offices — even representing the whole people before God as High Priest — such men were really servants of the Prince of this World, and in rebellion against God. Jesus must have seen the futility of any external deliverance of his people, such as that which the Zealots were desperately plotting, so long as this inward cancer of corruption was eating at their heart. So, loving his people, he declared war upon their national vices and false leaders rather than upon their foreign foes. Let the Holy People first be rescued from the usurping powers of Satan and restored to God, their sole rightful Sovereign; then they might once more face the kingdoms of this world unafraid. So reasoned Isaiah and Jeremiah, in their day; so, after the lapse of many centuries, reasoned John the Baptist and Jesus of Nazareth.

Why did Jesus locate the national center of rebellion against God's rule at Jerusalem? Partly of course because it was the political and religious capital; but partly also because it is in the city, more than in the country, that rebellion against God rises to heights of defiance. "God made the country, man made the city." There is evil and misery enough, God knows, in little villages and in the open country; but the dependence of man upon the regular rhythms of nature helps to preserve him from the illusion that he is the center of the universe, and can revolve around his own axis. If the countryman sometimes does not rise much above the level of the animals, at any rate he does not fall far below it. But in the city, man creates his own environment, and in that self-made microcosm elects himself king without a rival. He scoffs at the piety of rustic "boobs and yokels," and claims the right to do what he pleases, as he pleases. He throws aloft great sky-scraping towers, temples of self-esteem, which dwarf God's temples into insignificance. He creates filth, misery, and squalor such as nature knows nothing of, side by side with a glittering magnificence that holds itself coldly aloof from the lot of the poor. Here is the place for Satan to set up palatial headquarters, build up his political machine, and assemble his ward heelers. Let that back-country prophet make a scene if he likes, with his ragtag-and-bobtail band of rustic followers; he will make no impression here. Satan has only to sit tight and keep his political fences mended. Has he not Pilate and Herod, Annas and Caiaphas all on his side? Are not all the legions of Rome and all the learning of the rabbis equally at his disposal, to crush this ridiculous assault?

Nevertheless that ragged little band boldly enters the gates of Jerusalem and, with the sad-eyed Man of God at its head, presses on unopposed into the Temple precincts. *Why to the Temple?* Because there above all, in the midst of prayer and sacrifice, rather than in Herod's palace or the Antonia fortress, Jesus locates the stronghold of his enemies. He is not acting in anger, on a sudden impulse, when he releases the doves and overthrows the tables of the money-changers; he has surveyed the terrain quite coolly, and decided where and how to make his first attack. According to the Gospel of Mark (11:11), on the day of his arrival he simply does a bit of reconnoitering in the Temple, estimating the enemy's forces and checking up the surmise that they are indeed strongest just where one would least expect, in the House of God itself. Then he returns next day (Mark 11:15) to make a sudden show of force at just this strongest point — an attack so unexpected and so strategically sound that the Temple priesthood is completely discomfited and publicly humiliated.[5] They have no alternative but to surrender, or to counterattack. After several days of verbal warfare in the Temple courts, in which Jesus more than holds his own, but no acceptable peace terms are discovered, they do counterattack and bring about his arrest and execution — to their own ultimate undoing. Before Herod and Pilate, Jesus is silent; he has no immediate quarrel with them. Before the High Priest and the Sanhedrin, his real enemies, he is defiantly outspoken, predicting that though they kill him he will return on the clouds of heaven to establish that Rule of God which they have refused to accept (Matt. 26:64).

The tragedy of rebellion in the Temple is an eternally contemporary tragedy. Religious institutions are meant to be the light of the world; but when the light that is in them becomes darkness, how great is that darkness! When God's supposed representatives neither enter into His Kingdom nor permit others to enter; when God

---

[5] I am aware of the fact that the sequence of events during Jesus' last days in Jerusalem is not clear, but I offer the above as a plausible account, based upon Mark's Gospel.

knocks at the door of His own House and is refused admission, what worse thing can happen than this? Yet it happens repeatedly. Jesus' judgment that the Temple was in rebellion against God, and must be either purified or destroyed [6] before God could have His way again in Israel, was paralleled centuries later by Martin Luther's judgment upon the Church which claimed to be the only true Church of Christ; the Antichrist, for him, was not to be seen in the paynim Turks nor in the secular power of the Emperor, but in the successor of St. Peter at Rome.[7]

To Orthodox and Catholic minds, such judgments always seem blasphemous. Did not God promise His Church that the gates of hell should not prevail against her? Must not His chosen representatives succeed each other forever in legitimate Apostolic Succession, without a break, if the divine promise is to be fulfilled? So Annas and Caiaphas must have reasoned, when they rejected Jesus on the ground of God's promises to Abraham. To those ecclesiastical leaders who thus presume upon the divine promises, God always behaves like a

[6] For Jesus' prophecy of the destruction of the Temple he loved and sought to cleanse, cf. Matt. 26:61, 27:40, Mark 14:58, 15:29, John 2:19. See also Branscomb, *The Teachings of Jesus*, chap. xix, on "Jesus and the Temple."

[7] Another parallel, perhaps more palatable for Catholics (?) may be found in the case of Savonarola. Savonarola found that his attempt to reclaim Florence for God brought him into deadly conflict with Alexander VI, the Borgian Pope; and he denounced Alexander as an "antipope," who must either repent or be deposed before the Church could be restored to her purity. Neither Jesus nor Savonarola nor Luther preferred the *destruction* of religious institutions to their purification; but if purification did not come, destruction would.

Protestant. He deserts the old religious structure and erects a new one, declaring through His prophets that "the stone which the builders rejected, the same is become the head of the corner." Yet the divine impulse never is wholly dead in the old institution, nor does it wholly pass over into the new movement. While the Temple perishes, the Synagogue is revived and purified by the great tribulation of A.D. 70. While Northern Europe goes Protestant, Southern Europe experiences a Counter Reformation that makes an end of the iniquities of the Renaissance Popes. If our Protestantism is ever superseded by some new revolutionary religious movement, it will be inwardly renewed in the very process of resisting this innovation. Orthodoxy and Reform, Catholicism and Protestantism, continuity and change, are thus both included in the divine strategy.

It is not God's will to destroy any institution which has ever served His purposes, but rather to bring it to repentance and inward revitalization. Yet when God sent His Son, at the most critical moment in world history, to prepare the Church which was to save the world, he had first to fight the existing institutions of religion as though they were the very devil. He came to bring peace, to reconcile mankind to God and to each other; but the terms of peace were so repugnant to the official leaders of that day, both secular and religious, that they forced him to fight for his Great Peace, every inch of the way. Had he not loved mankind so deeply, he might have refused to fight; because he loved, with God's own infinite compassion, he had to be a fighter.

In the manner of his fighting, Jesus was merciful and chivalrous. Every act of war contained an offer of peace. He took the blows as far as possible upon his own body. Nonetheless, he effectively reduced his antagonists to confusion. By the unholiness of the passions which he unleashed in the breasts of high ecclesiastics, he unmasked the unreality of their religious pretensions, and showed the world that they were children of Satan. He wanted to redeem them, but if they would not let him do that, he could at least defeat them. He will always be victorious in that sense, at least, to the end of time. Those who oppose him may crucify him afresh, but in the end they have only two alternatives: to accept the terms of peace and reconciliation which he offers, and become his friends, or, if they insist on being his enemies, condemn themselves to endless misery and frustration.

The conception of Jesus as a great fighter and conqueror was widely prevalent in the first few centuries of the Christian era. In some early representations of the Crucifixion, Jesus appears as the Victor, even on the Cross. It was only later, when the "penal satisfaction" view of his atoning work became predominant, that he was represented as a crushed and broken Victim, pitiful in his helplessness. In recent years, Bishop Gustav Aulén's remarkable book, *Christus Victor*, has done much to revive the earlier view, and establish its right to be called the "classic" view, in contrast to all later theories. I am glad to admit my debt to Aulén, and my substantial agreement with his position. If I understand him rightly, he does not mean to suggest that this "classic" view, as presented in the Patristic writers and revived in Martin Luther, stands in flat *opposition* to the so-called "objective" and "subjective" views that were later developed by Anselm and Abélard, but only that it is more comprehensive and *inclusive*. It throws one great idea into bold relief which in other views tends to be ignored completely: the idea that Jesus fought and conquered the collective forces of evil and released mankind from captivity to them. But it by no means denies that the Cross of Christ is likewise an atonement for sin, and an invitation to repentance on the part of sinners.

Aulén himself, in contrast to some of his interpreters, stresses the fact that in the perspective of the whole work of Christ, God appears both as the Reconciler and the Reconciled, both as the God of love who offers the propitiatory sacrifice and as the God of wrath who needs to be propitiated. This implies that Jesus is both Victim and Victor, when the meaning of his Cross is surveyed from two different angles: a "saving Victim" for those who accept his sacrifice and the divine love it expresses; a Victor over those who continue to defy the divine wrath. Aulén describes his theory as "dualistic," because of the stress it lays upon the reality of an objective Kingdom of Evil; it might be even better to describe it as "three-cornered," since for Aulén the mediation of Christ involves a new relationship between *three* high contracting powers, instead of the *two* (God and man) with which most theories of the atonement have dealt: (1) a holy and loving God, (2) a powerful Kingdom of

Evil in rebellion against God, and (3) man, who is both a victim and a culprit — a victim of the powers of evil, and at the same time an accomplice in their rebellion, needing forgiveness as well as rescue. If this view of the significance of Jesus is true, our former views of him as Leader and Savior are not rendered untrue, but are taken up into a richer and more many-sided view, in which the note of Victory is dominant.

II. The continuing cosmic drama of darkness and light

One of the terms very properly used to describe Aulén's theory of the atonement is the term "dramatic." Everything in it revolves about *the cosmic drama of darkness and light*. It may help to bring all we have said about the meaning of Jesus' lifework into unity and perspective if we relate his figure to this cosmic drama — remembering, of course, that it is full of mysterious symbolism, but recognizing also that the highest religious truths are not expressible except in symbolic terms.

The symbolism of light and darkness, as expressions for good and evil, is very ancient. Primitive peoples, in the temperate and arctic zones, have naturally tended to identify all things good with the life-giving rays of the sun, on which their very existence depends, and all things evil with the forces of darkness and cold which creep over the earth in the late autumn and freeze up the sources of nourishment. Every winter, to their untutored imaginations, a dramatic battle is being fought between the forces of light and the forces of darkness, for the possession of the earth. When the days get shorter and shorter and when, even with slowly lengthening days, the cold continues to strengthen its hold, they hold their breaths in terror, and help the sun with all the magic spells they can muster, lest this time he should be decisively and permanently beaten by the powers of darkness.

When it comes to be understood at length that the seasons alternate as regularly as day and night, the symbolism shifts. Light and darkness become coeternal and coequal principles, the *Yang* and the *Yin* (as the Chinese call them). Forever and ever they circle round and round each other. The light is more active and creative, the darkness more passive and receptive. The light is the higher, better principle of the two, but each is indispensable to the other, and each generates the other. When the principle of light (*Yang*) predominates, there is a dark spot within it which is the germ of a coming era of darkness; when darkness (*Yin*) predominates, there is a germinal light spot within it from which a new age of light will develop. This way of looking at the world makes for philosophic calmness and an attitude of resignation to the inexorable forces of nature which tend to even things up in the end; but it does not encourage one to hope and work for any radical improvement in the world, or any decisive victory of good over evil.

The Christian symbolism of light and darkness is different from both of these older symbolisms. It is well expressed in a vision of George Fox, the Quaker seer: "I saw also that there was an ocean of darkness and death, but an infinite ocean of light and love, which flowed over the ocean of darkness: and in that also I saw the infinite love of God." [8] That is to say, the presence of evil in the world is not denied, but it is regarded (above all since the victory of Christ) as a secondary, subordinate, finite, temporal principle, whereas goodness is infinite and eternal like God himself, from whom it flows.

"God is light, and in Him is no darkness at all." [9] He is absolute and eternal goodness, and beside Him there is no coeternal principle with which He would need to co-operate in the work of creation. The world as it came from His creative hand in the beginning was "very good." [10] The fresh draught of life which each creature draws daily from its divine Source, to sustain its life until tomorrow, is also a draught of pure goodness, undefiled as a draught of pure water from a mountain spring. How evil can exist at all in such a world is a great mystery, unfathomable as the ocean; but as George Fox suggests, however deep may be the Mystery of Iniquity, the Mystery of Light is deeper still — rooted in infinity, whereas the other is rooted only in finitude.

We shall make no attempt at a philosophical solution of the problem of evil. Suffice it to say that no solution can be acceptable to the Christian mind which casts doubt upon the goodness of God, or makes any other principle coeternal with God, in order to cast the blame

[8] Fox, *Journal* (bicentenary edition, 1891), p. 19.
[9] I John 1:5.
[10] Genesis 1:31.

for evil upon it. Evil must be something which emerges in the course of the world process, contrary to God's will but dependent on His power, and vanishes again when His will is "done on earth as it is in heaven." How such a thing could be, we can only hint in terms of the symbolism of light and darkness:

A living plant, on the surface of the earth, derives its whole being ultimately from the sun. Not only the light and energy which it drinks in so copiously through its leaves on a warm spring day, but the nutriment which it absorbs through its roots, both are derived from the sun; for earth itself, with all it contains, sprang originally from the sun and has depended on its parent ever since. A plant, then, is pure coagulated radiance from above, compact of sun-dust, sun-vapor, and sunlight. But every plant has a spontaneity of its own, whereby it uses the common gift of radiance from above in a manner peculiar to itself. Some plants turn solar energy into flowers that reflect the colors of the solar spectrum, and fruits that sustain life; others turn it into poison. There is one plant which literally turns life-giving sunshine into deadly nightshade. Without light it could not be at all, could not go on existing for more than a short space of time; but its works are works of darkness.

It is so also with mankind. Man is compact of light, and light alone; there is nothing dark or evil in his original composition. But noblest of all the good gifts which God has showered upon His human creatures is a gift of spontaneity far higher than a plant's, a veritable *power to create* which, within finite bounds, images the infinite power of the Creator. This creative gift is a gift of light, but man can use it for works of darkness. He probably began so using it as soon as he became a man, as soon as the Image of God was imprinted upon him, as soon as that creative intelligence appeared in him which distinguished him from other animals. He tripped and fell over the very first step that led him up above the level of brutality, and he has done the same at every step on the way from savagery to higher civilization. Every discovery, every invention, every achievement of men's creative intelligence has been to some degree perverted to evil ends, and become a work of darkness.

This is not all the fault of Adam, or *Pithecanthropus Erectus*, or whoever the first true man may have been. Every man is in a very real sense his own Adam, and has his own temptation and fall; for every man is a new creation of God, bearing within him a freshly imparted creative spark, to use or to misuse. When he misuses it, however great the external forces that drove him to pervert his powers from their true source and goal, he knows he was partly responsible for the tragedy. But when my works of darkness, and yours, and other men's, and perhaps other spiritual beings' as well, are compounded with one another and mingled with the works of our predecessors, the result is something more terrible than any one of us could create by himself. There is gradually built up, in the midst of God's fair earth, a "City of Dreadful Night," walled about with thick darkness, so that God's light cannot get in.

The walls of this city, in their original substance, are

made of light, and its inhabitants are all children of light in the root of their being. Should the God of Light withdraw His support for a moment, the walls would tumble down and the inhabitants would perish. But out of God's own radiance there has been created a temporary barrier of defense against Him, which suffices for that purpose. Darkness may be but an evanescent phenomenon in God's world, thinly veiling the light of which it is composed; but when this perishable fabric is woven stoutly together into evil habits, evil ideas and tendencies, evil institutions, it becomes thick and palpable enough to shut out the light; and behind this wall of darkness there springs up a revolt of creation against its Source, a kind of gangster rule which supersedes the Rule of God in these benighted slums. Then men are *born* into such slums and corrupted by the foul atmosphere, so that they never realize their destiny as children of light.

If God is truly good, He cannot be content to do nothing about this. The Christian "Good News" is that He has done something, something costly and effective, to break the power of darkness over mankind. He has come down, in the person of His well-beloved Son, into the very midst of the prison which men have built for themselves — not only to release the prisoners, but to make a breach in the prison walls and let the light stream in. To be sure, God has always been coming into His world. By His Word of Wisdom and Power, the same divine power whereby the world was created, He continually makes life and light to spring up in the midst of death and darkness. Even within the City of Dreadful

Night that men have built, "The light is still shining in darkness, for the darkness has never put it out." [11] But this was not enough — not even when prophetic voices were inspired to cry out in many lands, bearing witness to the light. There followed therefore what Berdyaev calls God's "second act." The first great act of God was when He poured Himself generously forth in creation and continued to sustain what He had created. The second act was when He came in humble human guise into the world He had created, as the "Suffering and Sacrificial God" who "shares the bitter destiny of the world and of man" [12] in order to win them back to unity with Himself.

Such an act on the part of God demands as its counterpart the freely surrendered will of a human being. Jesus was such a human being as God needed to find free entrance into humanity. God's uncreated light took flesh in him, and shone into the darkest places precisely because they were the darkest, to bring "deliverance to captives and recovery of sight to the blind." Not only did he deliver captives out of dark places, but he delivered himself up as a captive to the Prince of Darkness, in order to break Satan's power over others. [13] When the

[11] John 1:5 (Goodspeed's translation).

[12] Berdyaev, *The Destiny of Man*, p. 133. In chapter v, I am describing this as the "third step" in God's approach to man, enumerating "moral government" as a second step, between creation (1) and redemption (3). Berdyaev, who has a low opinion of law and government as instruments of divine providence, does not think this phase of God's action worth mentioning.

[13] We find it very hard, of course, to penetrate Jesus' motives for allowing himself to be entrapped by his enemies, since we do not

multitude with swords and staves came to arrest Jesus by night in the Garden of Gethsemane, he made a strange remark: "This is your hour," he said, "and the power of darkness." [14] Apparently he took them as representatives of a superhuman Power of Darkness, the center of all the evil with which mankind was afflicted, and found it appropriate that the representatives of such a Power should seize their prey by night. From that moment on, until the great reversal of Easter morning, Jesus was in the hands of the Enemy, and the Prince of Darkness reigned temporarily over God's earth. The Gospel narratives report, as though it were a fact of preternatural significance, that on the day of the crucifixion there was "darkness over all the land" [15] from noon until three o'clock. Under that pall of darkness, Jesus suffered his last agonies, cried out to God in horror and desolation of spirit, and dropped his head upon his breast in apparently final defeat. The older liturgical churches still commemorate this period of Satan's triumph

---

think in the same imagery. We think of disease medically, he thought of it as a work of Satan; we think of the corrupt ring of ecclesiastical politicians who opposed him, while he saw behind their opposition the work of a superhuman Adversary. I think it probable that Jesus consciously gave himself up to Satan, "as a ransom for many" (Mark 10:45), when he surrendered outside Gethsemane. Whatever Jesus consciously intended, I believe that through the arrest and crucifixion of His beloved Son, God administered a mighty and decisive blow to the power of evil in human life.

[14] Luke 22:53.

[15] Luke 23:44. I do not assume of course that all the portents reported by the Gospels are correctly reported or rightly interpreted. But the whole narrative testifies to the deep conviction of the Early Church that *Satan temporarily triumphed over Christ.*

with impressive ceremonies. I quote from a Roman Catholic description [16] of the liturgy for Good Friday and Holy Saturday:

> Year after year the sacred liturgy leads us step by step along the *via dolorosa* and up the slope of Golgotha to this darkness, this parting cry, and this enveloping void. On Good Friday night the Catholic world sits in a darkened church and hears the mournful chants of Tenebrae and the wailings of Jeremias the prophet. Purple veils hide the marble forms of saints and angels from view. Not a single linen cloth is upon the altars. The sanctuary lamp is dark; the holy water fonts are dry and the tabernacle is empty, its door thrown wide as though by a vandal hand. Slowly one by one the thirteen candles on the tripod are extinguished. At last all is blackness. All is silence, too, except for the sob of the *Miserere*. A numbness ensues which sinks finally into unconsciousness and the Catholic world sleeps.
>
> At length Time begins to reassert itself. There is a slight stir like a wind moving high up in the arches of the nave. Footsteps are heard as a little group of vested figures makes its way from the sacristy to the door of the church. They are like men returning valiantly to a countryside which has been ravaged by fire and earthquake.
>
> They must begin at the very beginning — they must reconstruct civilization from its very foundation. So they strike a flint against steel until the sparks ignite a bit of charcoal. Then, calling upon the Author of all light to bless this new-born fire, they light one branch of a three-branched candle, and a deacon chants, "Lumen Christi."

[16] Brenton McCormack in *Our Sunday Visitor* for April 10, 1938.

The Light of Christ was not extinguished by the Power of Darkness which apparently snuffed it out; that is the Good News on which the whole Christian message is fundamentally based. Christian imagination has richly embroidered this amazing story of a divine Defeat and Surrender, that led at last to a divine Victory. Christ has been represented in Christian legend as descending into hell to ransom the captives of the Prince of Darkness. He goes as a defeated prisoner of war, so to speak, but his grim captor presently discovers that he cannot hold this Prisoner. Clad in light, Christ moves at will in Satan's dark domains. He preaches to the "spirits in prison" and liberates the righteous patriarchs from the limbo where they have been awaiting his advent. The devil is cheated! Mankind is ransomed by Christ's captivity to the powers of darkness, but the sinless Christ cannot long be "holden of death," and reascends to the right hand of God.

I for one value this ancient Christian legend, and I do not bracket the descent into hell when I encounter it in the Apostles' Creed. It seems to me characteristic of the real Spirit of Jesus to go to the very bottom of the evil in the world, wherever that bottom may be, and to break the power of evil in the world by suffering that power in its most infernal intensity. But I do not think it necessary to speak in terms of a dubious infernal geography, or to bring literal horned devils and winged demons into the picture, in order to state the nature and effect of the divine Victory that was won on Calvary.

What happened, as I see it, was this: In and through His well-beloved Son, God made decisive military "contact" with the forces of evil that opposed His sovereign right to rule the world. Having located the center of these rebellious forces in the spot most sacred to His Chosen People, the Temple at Jerusalem, God summoned the ecclesiastical leaders of this hitherto unconscious rebellion to choose between accepting His will as defined by his High Plenipotentiary, and openly flouting His will by laying violent hands upon His envoy. When they chose the latter course, their doom was sealed; for in an all-out attack against God and His anointed, they were bound to expose their vulnerable flank — the unrighteousness of their cause — and defeat themselves by their own victory. Nothing has ever so exposed the hatefulness of evil, and its ultimate weakness, as the Cross of Jesus. The spectacle of divine love, courageous unto death, vilely spat upon and contemned by human self-will, delivers men from the power and prestige of evil as nothing else can do. Evil veiled in good intentions is seductive; but here at last, mocking the divine Sufferer on the Cross, is evil in its nakedness; and it is hideous, nauseating, *powerless to command men's allegiance*. Evil still exists in the world, and still has power to slay the righteous; but the power of evil was decisively broken when it overreached itself against God's righteousness in Christ, betraying its essential loathsomeness and essential weakness. Battles against evil still have to be fought; but the battle of Calvary was the center of human history, and the turning point in the cosmic struggle of light and darkness. When Christ fell into the hands of the Prince of This World, it was the darkest day that ever dawned — for the hosts of darkness.

Just how the disciples of Jesus became convinced of the fact of his victorious Resurrection will never be quite clear; the accounts of it in the New Testament are too inconsistent to be fully reconciled; but it is perfectly clear that it changed everything for them. Their bold little expedition against the ruling powers in Jerusalem had ended in a defeat that was a complete rout. Hoping to the end that God might intervene to save their Leader and support his cause, they were utterly disillusioned by his capture and execution, and lost all faith in his mission. They had hoped "that it had been he which should have redeemed Israel";[17] but evidently it was only another one of those false mirages by which Israel had been so often deceived. So the whole movement Jesus had led broke up in disorderly retreat. A few weeks later, we find the movement reconstituted, reunited in spirit with its ascended Leader, and celebrating his coming victory over the world as though it were already achieved. Ever since, the great victory shout of the Christian movement has been the Easter antiphon: "Christ is risen! — He is risen indeed!"

III. How Jesus' victory helps us now

From the beginning, the Christian community has always looked back to *an achieved victory* foreshadowing

[17] Luke 24:21.

a future victory. On the strength of Christ's conquest of
the powers of death and hell, which overreached and
overthrew themselves in the endeavor to hold him in
their clutches, the Church has confidently prophesied
his future victory over all the ills that darken the face
of God's earth. While she awaits the beginning of his
future public reign, she lives in the power of his present
reign in the hearts of those who are his. For those who
are his, and live in his power, "the darkness is past, and
the true light now shineth." [18] The "rulers of the darkness of this world" [19] can neither hurt nor affright them,
for Christ has already won a first decisive victory over
these powers, and armored his followers against all
their fiery darts.

The final victory of Christ over the kingdoms of this
world has been long delayed. What the apostles hoped
to see before they died has not yet come to pass; nor do
we expect it ever to come to pass in the form they im-
agined. We do not look for the day when "the heavens
shall pass away with a great noise, and the elements shall
melt with fervent heat." [20] But if we have penetrated far
into the meaning of the strategic attack which our Lord
and Leader made upon the forces of evil in the world we
cannot help feeling that the early Christians were
right in their conviction that his decisive initial victory
guarantees a more sweeping public victory in the future,
and an eternal victory when time shall be no more.

[18] I John 2:8.
[19] Eph. 6:12.
[20] II Peter 3:10.

Karl Heim has embodied this persistent Christian conviction in a striking simile. When the lightning has flashed,
he remarks, we know that the thunderclap must come.
Lightning and thunder are the same event manifesting
itself in two different media. They occur simultaneously;
but we perceive the lightning at once through the swift
ether, while we perceive the thunder later through the
slower medium of the atmosphere. In the medium of the
Spirit, the victory of Christ registered its effects with
lightning swiftness in the gathering of a new community
freely united to him as its head, and typifying the new
world order that is to be. In the more resistant medium
of human institutional life, the same victory registers its
effects far more slowly. We still are waiting for the
thunderclap. Whole civilizations have arisen which have
been permeated by Christ's influence like yeast in dough.
They have lapsed again into secularism after a brief
period of glorious outflowering; but if Christ's initial
victory means what the New Testament says it means,
there can be no final overthrow of his Kingdom; some
day he must triumph in the world at large as he has
already triumphed in the hearts of believers.

I am inclined to amend Heim's simile, in the light of
Christianity's experience with civilizations and social
orders. Perhaps the public victory of Christ is like
thunder *in the mountains:* a long series of crashing reverberations after a single lightning flash. We have
already heard the first two or three of these reverberations, in the mighty effects that Christianity has already
had upon Western civilization. Perhaps the next will

coincide with the founding of a Christian world culture upon the ruins of our present decadent industrialism.[21] Perhaps that one conclusive thunderclap for which our premillenarian friends still listen will be heard — like the "Lost Chord" — only in eternity, where God garners up the harvests of all ages.

While we wait and work for Christ's future public victory, we are helped in many ways, even now, by his historic victory on Calvary, to which the Early Church bears witness:

1. *Jesus' victory over his adversaries delivers us from craven fear of the modern adversaries of Christianity.* We face a scene of social chaos which fills us, not without reason, with grave apprehensions. But there is one sort of apprehension to which no Christian, since the first Easter and Pentecost, should ever give way: the apprehension lest goodness and truth should finally be unseated in the universe, and evil reign supreme. In the face of the growing power of violence in our time, *that* apprehension is seriously felt by many of our contemporaries. Since Christ suffered and conquered, it is possible to pronounce this dread surmise a pure superstition — as inexcusable for moderns as the fear that this winter the sun may not return from his southward trek. That was not a superstition for our savage ancestors who knew no better; but it has become a superstition ever since the regularity of the seasons was discovered. It was not superstitious for the disciples to flee in terror

[21] On the prospects for a Christian world culture, see my recent book, *Can Christianity Save Civilization?* (Harper & Brothers, 1940.)

when Jesus was arrested and crucified; but it is superstitious for us, who have seen the outcome of the crucifixion and seen the risen Christ at work for two thousand years — for us, it is superstitious to fear that the delaying of the Kingdom of God means the possible triumph of evil. Evil has done its worst against Christ, and failed; thenceforth we ought all to know that in any final showdown it will defeat itself again. That does not mean that we and our kind will come off victorious in every battle with our enemies. We are not embodiments of pure righteousness, and our enemies are not imps of hell. Against us and our kind, wars and revolutions may succeed; but against Christ, to win is always to lose, and to lose is to win. Christ abides in our midst. It is possible to crucify him afresh. But from each fresh crucifixion he must rise again as Victor, for the eternal God is in him.

2. *The campaign against the Prince of This World which Jesus started is still sweeping on, and its momentum supports us in our struggle with contemporary evils.* It very nearly was abandoned, when Jesus fell into the hands of his enemies; but his unexpected triumph over death and humiliation rallied his scattered forces, and sent them forth upon a world-wide mission which has never ceased. Often it has seemed as though the Christian movement had lost its aggressive character, and settled down into defensive isolation; but the appearance has always proved deceitful. There have been truces and temporary working agreements between the followers of Jesus and the Prince of This World, but

no final peace. There have been forms of Christianity which have achieved social respectability, through confining their activity to approved forms of rescue work and general uplift, but any privileged class which thinks it has safely domesticated the Christian movement as a whole is making a dangerous mistake.

The attitude of Christianity toward poverty, disease, vice, crime, and injustice is not merely charitable and ameliorative, but revolutionary. It regards these evils as contrary to God's will, and seeks therefore to *eradicate* them, not merely to *mitigate* them, while at the same time trying to *convert* rather than to *destroy* their human representatives. In modern times, social science has put a wealth of information at the disposal of Christian revolutionaries, which tends to drive home the lesson that prevention of evil is better than cure, and the reconstruction of a bad social system is better than the perennial rescue of its victims. Rescue, redemption, forgiveness, will always be characteristic forms of Christian action, but *aggressive attack upon vested wrong* is equally characteristic. No hater of injustice need feel that he stands alone, if he is a member of this movement, and an effective participant in its unending campaign. When "tired radicals" became disillusioned with the results of other forms of revolutionary action, there is still Christianity to fall back upon, as A. J. Muste has eloquently testified. Other agencies of reform and revolution are necessary beside the Christian Church; but the Church should provide central inspiration, drive, and guidance to them all, as her aims are more far-reaching than any.

It is a great pity that Marxism and other modern revolutionary movements have been driven into opposition to their best potential ally, by the conservatism of certain privileged Christian groups.

3. *The strategy of Jesus suggests the lines along which modern Christian strategy needs to be developed.* The Christian pacifists are right when they appeal to Jesus as one who defines not only the *purpose and goal* but the characteristic *methods and tactics* of the Christian enterprise. They are right in their contention that if we do not employ Christian *means* we shall hardly attain to Christian *ends*. They are right in their observation that modern warfare has become what Gerald Heard calls *an instrument of maximum imprecision*, entailing all kinds of unintended, undesired evils at every step, often destroying what it is intended to preserve and preserving what it is intended to destroy.

During the present world conflict, there has been an encouraging advance toward mutual comprehension between Christian pacifists and nonpacifists, which may eventually bring us to approximate agreement as to what constitutes an effective Christian strategy.

On the one hand, pacifists now usually admit that some form of fighting is part of our Christian duty, since Christianity is not only a redemptive movement but also a movement for social justice, and the conversion of a few unjust men is not enough to make an end of any form of injustice. Whereas Henry Hodgkin's pacifist strategy, in his *Christian Revolution*, fought shy of every form of mass pressure and political action, his successors in the Fellowship of Reconciliation are now almost unanimously in favor of that form of "nonviolent coercion" practiced by Mr. Gandhi in his struggle for Indian *swaraj*. They see in this a legitimate development of Jesus' own characteristic strategy: a method of fighting that holds out at every moment an offer of friendship and reconciliation to the enemy; a method whereby the attacker takes the blows upon himself so far as possible ("self-suffering"), and the enemy is made to defeat himself by overreaching himself, finally confessing defeat with gladness and relief rather than to persist in what his own conscience tells him to be cruel wrong. Most of them, however, would admit that this method is not yet perfected as an instrument of national policy. Mr. Gandhi's advice to the Jews and Czechs as to what they should have done against Hitler was so palpably impracticable that many pacifists now appreciate the dilemma: *either take no action, as a nation, to check rapidly mounting injustice in world politics, or check it by the clumsy military means which are all that we now have at our disposal.*

Nonpacifists, on their part, may now gratefully accept the new pacifist definition of the problem of Christian strategy: *not*, "to fight or not to fight," but "how to fight effectively, as not beating the air." They may admit the ineffectiveness of modern warfare, of which both belligerents in the present world conflict are so evidently conscious. (Think of the "pulling of punches" in the opening months; the German attempt to avoid a "war of position" and end the war quickly by Blitzkrieg tactics; the mounting desperation on both sides when war became "total," and began to spread uncontrollably.) While believing in the temporary necessity of these cruel and wasteful tactics, Christian nonpacifists will join with Christian pacifists in combating the worst of the hazards of war: the influence of vengeful passions upon the minds of those who make the peace. And they will hope for the speedy return of the day when they can show Christian mercy as well as Christian righteousness toward their present military opponents.

It is possible that Christian pacifists and nonpacifists may between them accomplish what neither party could accomplish alone, in the present historic emergency. Nonpacifists will help to prosecute the war, throwing their weight on the side more likely to bring about a just and durable peace, but refusing to hate or slander the other side. They will have more influence than pacifists in the shaping of the peace treaty. But if they succeed in setting up a framework of international order sufficient to restrain the present chaos of competing selfish interests, the working and progressive readjustment of this new order may well depend upon the inventive genius of pacifists, in perfecting a new instrument of precision for the redressing of social wrongs without violence. John Foster Dulles in *War, Peace and Change* has shown that it is not enough to establish a temporarily just and workable equilibrium in the world, unless provision is made for the subsequent peaceful settlement of new disputes. I doubt whether any international court, or any sort of legal machinery, will be sufficient to solve the problem of peaceful change, unless we have the aid of disciplined bands of men who care so much for social justice and hate war so furiously that they are willing to suffer much to bring about the release of those social pressures that will wreck any social order if allowed to accumulate too long.

May it not be that in the new international order established at the close of this war, active pacifists of the Gandhi type will have an opportunity to extend Gandhi's methods beyond the bounds of a single nation? Haya de la Torre has already done something of the sort with the *Apra* movement in South America. The trials of this war may develop new skills among Christian pacifists working in favorable limited areas or in such frightfully difficult areas as Continental Europe — where, nevertheless, it is already evident that terrorism is futile. Much can be learned by pacifists from the extraordinarily philosophic way in which China is carrying on her part in the war — putting "national reconstruction" alongside "resistance" as perhaps the more important of the two co-ordinate factors in a great social struggle. Is it too much to hope that out of these suggestions and experiments, with the continued inspiration of the Spirit of Jesus, there may at length evolve an instrument of national and international policy capable of maintaining friendly and redemptive relations with the enemy even in the midst of conflict, capable of suspending hostilities occasionally without suspicion of weakness or cowardice, and capable of negotiating a satisfactory peace before the two antagonists have battered each other to bloody pulp?

If and when this comes to pass, Jesus our Eternal Contemporary will have won his most spectacular victory, to date, and the Prince of Darkness will have suffered his greatest defeat. We do not know whether any such events may occur in our time, but in Jesus' name we dare to hope and pray and work — both patiently and energetically — for this and many another coming victory of light over darkness. And while we work and wait, we are not disconsolate, for we know that each human soul tempered in the long conflict with evil is an end in itself, richly worth Christ's struggle, even if (*par impossible*) the hosts of light should meet with final defeat. Such souls, garnered up in God's granary of the ages, would be harvest enough for this earth to have produced, even if the City of Dreadful Night should continue to get the better of the City of God, to the end of history. To have fought in the Church Militant, and afterwards to be received into the Church Triumphant, along with all the heroes of faith (Hebrews 11), should be reward enough for any Christian.

Chapter Five

Who Then Is Jesus That Is Called the Christ?

THROUGHOUT the pages of this book, we have been pursuing the clue to a mystery. We have been trying to understand how Jesus of Nazareth, who lived nearly two thousand years ago, can be our own living contemporary. That Jesus is still an active power in our midst is a conviction that has grown upon us, as we have considered the different aspects of his work. He is still our Leader and Guide, who holds our confidence and loyalty as no contemporary religious leader or political master can hold it for long. He is still our Savior, who rescues us from our guilty alienation, and restores us to right relationship with God and fellow men, at dreadful cost to himself and the God he represents. He is still our Champion, who wages victorious warfare on our behalf against the powers of evil that have usurped the government of God's good earth; or, in the Biblical terms which have become classic in theology, he is still our Prophet, Priest, and King.

One way of explaining this extraordinary fact is to point to the living chain of his followers and "ambassadors," who connect us with him across the centuries. Through such a living chain, his influence reaches us in distant times and places without fading out as it would inevitably do in a less electric medium. A stone thrown into a pond creates waves which are practically imperceptible before they reach the shore. A shout thrown into the air re-echoes for a few moments, then dies away forever. But the life of Jesus, sacrificially thrown into the lives of his disciples, kindled there a new life that has never died away, and never will. His leadership made fishers of men out of fishermen; his forgiveness made them forgiving, and his Cross inspired them to take up their crosses; his Victory encouraged them to defy the Prince of This World, and carry on the battle against evil without fear of "them that kill the body, and after that have no more that they can do." From generation to generation, this Apostolic Succession has been perpetuated, less by the official laying-on of hands than by the personal contact of parents upon children, leaders and teachers upon followers and pupils. When fatness and complacency have threatened to destroy the vital continuity of this living chain, persecution and martyrdom have restored it.

This is surely a great part of the truth, but Christian faith is never wholly content with it. Christians are conscious of a more immediate communion with their Lord and Master than that which they have with him through their predecessors in the living chain. It is as though Christ came down to them directly and vertically, from overhead, and not merely horizontally, through his earthly historical influence. It is as though his grace and truth were active throughout the universe, his presence everywhere, and not merely where his name is named by those who call themselves his people. Every doctrine of the Person of Christ, every attempt to answer the question, "Whom say ye that I am?" from Peter's confession at Cæsarea Philippi down to the most elaborate Christological speculations, is inspired by this mysterious sense that he is *from above*.

Our own confession will be respectful of that inevitable remainder of mystery which will always baffle Christian thought when it moves in these regions; but it will light up the mystery as far as possible by appealing to the whole range of Christian doctrine, from Creation to the Last Judgment, especially the two basic ideas which run through the whole of it as its warp and woof: *the idea of God and the idea of man*. All that we know about God, all that we know about man, and all that we know about the relationship between man and God at its best, we apply to the interpretation of the mysterious person of Jesus, the meeting point of God and man.

That is not to say that we first arrive at an idea of God and an idea of man, quite independently of Jesus, and then drape these ideas externally upon him, as though he were an inert lay figure. The process of Christian thought is more complicated than that. The Christian idea of God and the Christian idea of man are both very largely derived from the life and teachings of Jesus; and the elements thus derived are the most precious elements.[1] This being the case, Christian theology has to

---

[1] It has always been felt to be an impiety to measure Jesus' deity or Jesus' humanity by any non-Christian conception of God or man. For example, there is a common pagan notion that God is very big

reason in a circle, so to speak, if it is to think about Jesus. It starts inevitably with the revelation of God and man which he has brought, for this is the center of our Christian faith. About this center, it then organizes all that is known of God and man from any other source.[2] Then it turns back and views the figure of Jesus in the light of this comprehensive doctrine of God and man, not wholly derived from him and so capable of illuminating him. This is indeed a circular process of reasoning, proceeding from Jesus and coming back to Jesus, but it is not a *"vicious* circle." Each time the Christian mind makes the circuit from Jesus out to the totality of religious knowledge, and back to him again, it returns enriched with new insight.

Let us make the experiment, and see if it is not so. We have been concentrating our attention upon Jesus and his influence; now let us turn our attention to the God he served and the human race he renewed, and see what light they cast upon *who he is*.

I. Jesus as the incarnate Word of God

Jesus is the wisdom and power of God, the redemptive mercy of God, coming forth "in the form of a servant" for the salvation of mankind. The possibility of such a *coming forth*, such a *coming down* of God to the level

---

and proud, which would rule out the possibility that He could appear in a little child, or come into Jerusalem "lowly, and riding upon an ass," or die upon a Cross of shame; but the revelation of God in Jesus simply overturns this common notion, and makes a laughingstock of it.

[2] Some, like Karl Barth, refuse to recognize any other source, and so lapse into dogmatism.

of His creatures, to do them good, is essential to the Hebrew and Christian idea of God; there is from all eternity a manward motion in the depths of God's being, a motion which apart from the Incarnation would remain abortive and defeated.

Some conceptions of God (Aristotle's, for example) imply that the Creator is completely self-sufficient apart from His creation — so much so that He appears to be indifferent to the world, and absorbed in self-contemplation. Christian thought has been considerably and unwholesomely affected at times by this notion that God's perfection implies His complete and unqualified "by-himselfness" (*aseitas*). But in Hebrew thought, above all in the teaching of Jesus, God's perfection is seen rather in the unstinted generosity with which He pours forth blessings upon His creatures, even upon the thankless and the evil. Always, everywhere, it is His nature to come forth into His creation, humbly and lovingly, to sustain and to heal, if His creatures will but open the door to the august Guest who comes as a beggar and knocks.

There are three major steps in God's approach to His creatures.

1. In *creation* itself, God comes forth from Himself by His creative Word of Wisdom, imparts His Image to all that He creates (above all to man, the highest of earthly creatures), and stays in the world to sustain what He has made, moment by moment, while at the same time He remains above His creation, as its transcendent Source.

2. In His *moral government* of His creatures, God draws a step nearer. He does not leave them to their own devices, standing aside like an umpire to see what they will do with their God-given powers, and rewarding or punishing them accordingly. Without coercing their freedom (the highest of His gifts to them) He guides them by His prophetic Word of Wisdom. This guiding Word came to Israel through the Law and the Prophets, to other peoples through their sages and philosophers, whose ears were in varying degrees attuned to the divine speech.

3. When God's prophetic Word labors in vain, as often happens, God is not defeated. He still sits aloft upon His transcendent Throne of Judgment, and in due season brings down earth's mighty from their seats if they persistently refuse to listen to His messengers. But He is grieved to be thrust back into the role of Judge and Executioner. It is His deepest will to re-create and redeem that which has gone wrong, not to destroy it. So in His work of redemption God takes a momentous third step, which brings Him all the way into the very heart of His creation, the soul of man. Through a willing and prepared human being, chosen from a chosen people, God enters into humanity while still remaining above humanity. In Jesus of Nazareth, God's creative, prophetic, redemptive Word "was made flesh and dwelt among us, and we beheld His glory, glory as of the only begotten of the Father, full of grace and truth" (John 1:14).

When the idea of the "Word made flesh" was first

clearly stated in the prologue to the Gospel of John, it already had a long history. The distinction between God *hidden* and God *revealed*, God *above* His creation and God active *in* His creation by His Word of Wisdom and Power, had long been familiar to Jewish thought. It seems to have been through contact with Greek speculation that Jewish thought developed this distinction, for it is in the late "wisdom literature" (written after the subjection of Palestine by the Greek Seleucid kings) that it is first consistently observed. In the Book of Proverbs, for example, Wisdom is personified, and speaks words that remind us of the opening verse of the Gospel of John; [3] while in The Wisdom of Solomon (an apocryphal book coming from the Greek period) Wisdom is described in terms that remind us of the Apostle Paul's description of Christ: "the breath of the power of God . . . a spotless mirror of the activity of God . . . a likeness of His goodness." [4]

What is new in Paul and John is their application of this ancient Jewish idea to the Man Christ Jesus. Jewish thought already recognized in God's creative, prophetic Word of Wisdom an eternal "Son of God" (i.e., a power coming forth from God into the world), but it saw this power best revealed in God's commandments

[3] "The Lord possessed me *in the beginning* of His ways, before His works of old. . . . When He prepared the heavens, *I was there.* . . . When He appointed the foundations of the earth, then *I was by Him, as one brought up with Him.* . . . The Lord by Wisdom hath founded the earth; by Understanding hath He prepared the Heavens" (Proverbs 8:22, 27, 29, 30, and 3:19).

[4] Wisdom of Solomon 7:25, 26; cf. I Cor. 1:24, II Cor. 3:18.

given to Israel through Moses and the prophets. Paul and John [5] saw God's eternal Word more evidently present in the Man Jesus, God's Messenger of Redemption, than in all Creation and all Scripture apart from him. The same divine wisdom and power whereby God made the heavens and the earth, whereby He enlightened the prophets and governed the nations, now lived a human life in Jesus, spoke through human lips, and even (though this was "foolishness to the Greeks" [6]) died a human death! In the lowly Man of Nazareth, the immortal and invisible Son of God had been sent forth on a redemptive mission to mortal men, and in that human face crowned with thorns could be seen "glory as of the only begotten of the Father, full of grace and truth."

Here already in the New Testament, except for two ambiguities, is the idea of the Incarnation found afterward in the Nicene Creed and the Nicene Fathers: ". . . for us men and for our salvation," God "became as we are that He might make us as He is."

1. One ambiguity concerns the relationship between God's Son or Word, and God Himself. In the Pauline Christology (e.g., Philippians 2:5-11, Colossians 1:13-20) it is not unambiguously clear whether the celestial being who "thought not equality with God a thing to

[5] When I say "Paul and John" I do not mean to imply that the Christologies expressed in the Pauline and Johannine writings are the work of two individual Christian thinkers. The two greatest Christological passages in their writings (the prologue to the Gospel of John, and Philippians 2:5-11) are almost certainly *hymns of the Early Church*, reflecting the faith of the multitudes of common Christians, and not merely the speculations of two eminent thinkers.

[6] I Cor. 1:23.

be grasped at" [7] was only the "first-born of every creature" [8] (as Arius long afterward insisted) or "of one
substance with the Father" (as Athanasius and the Council of Nicaea declared). The Gospel of John's statement
of the Incarnation is classical for all later Christian
thought, because it makes clear that the Word which
became flesh in Jesus was not only "in the form of God"
and "with God" from the beginning, but essentially
"*was* God" — a statement consistent with the strictest
Jewish monotheism.

2. The other ambiguity concerns the relationship
between the divine Presence in Jesus and his human nature. Here the Fourth Gospel takes a step backward
from Paul. It represents the Man Jesus as wearing and
exercising the divine attributes of omniscience and om-
nipotence that were his before his birth. He not only
was the divine Word of Wisdom, he *knew* it all the
time: "Before Abraham was, I am." The human limitations that he wore were a mere garb; in short, his life
was not a genuine *incarnation* at all, in spite of what the
prologue says, but only a *theophany*, like Jehovah's "appearing" to Abraham in the plains of Mamre, or to
Moses on the Mount. I share Professor Knox's enthusiasm for Paul's doctrine that in Jesus God "became
veritable man," and I agree with Knox that whenever
this "really great idea" has been lost, through the
"qualification" of the complete humanity of Jesus, Christian thought has receded from its high-water mark, and

[7] Phil. 2:6.
[8] Col. 1:15.

fallen into confusion.[9] The only fully Christian idea of the Incarnation is that in Jesus *God Himself* (as the prologue to the Fourth Gospel says) *became fully human* (as Paul says) and so entered irrevocably into the time-process, *while nevertheless remaining "God over all, blessed forever."* Only in such a conception is the idea of *God coming forth from Himself to bless His creatures* fully carried through. This is essentially the position taken later by the Councils of Nicaea and Chalcedon — with the aid of certain Greek philosophic distinctions quite foreign to Paul and John.[10]

To believe in Jesus as God's incarnate Word of Wisdom and Power is not to disparage other manifestations of divine wisdom and power. The wisdom of the Greek philosophers and the sages of the ancient East, the amazing power of God's ordering intelligence as exhibited in the universe of modern science, from atom to cosmos — from these and many other sources, we have a many-sided knowledge of God that is not directly derived from God's self-revelation in Jesus. For every scrap of such knowledge, we must be grateful. But God's deepest wisdom and power are revealed in the humble life and tragic death of Jesus; and all other knowledge of God must be reconciled somehow with this. If that be not easy, it is the fault of our limited hearts and minds, not the fault of God. He has drawn as near to us, in Jesus, as it is possible for Him to come without destroy-

[9] Knox, *The Man Christ Jesus*, pp. 89, 90. See the whole section beginning on p. 82.

[10] For my own attitude toward the creeds of Nicaea and Chalcedon — an attitude quite different from Knox's — see Appendix C.

ing us. "No man shall see God and live. . . ." "No man hath seen God at any time; the only begotten Son, which is in the bosom of the Father, He hath declared Him" (Ex. 33:20; John 1:18).

II. Jesus as founder and head of a new humanity

Jesus is the One through whom the redemptive power of God found entrance into the rebellious City of Man, and began to renew and reorder the whole human race. In this idea of a new humanity, reborn and restored in Jesus the Second Adam, the whole Christian doctrine of man culminates, as the Christian doctrine of God culminates in the idea of the Incarnation.

There are three stages in man's relationship with God, according to Christian teaching; and they correspond exactly to the three steps in God's approach to man.

1. In man's *state of integrity* (i.e., so long as man retains his childlike innocence, and his nature is not corrupted by sin) he bears the image of his Creator so clearly mirrored in his soul that Jesus looking upon a human child could say, "Of such is the Kingdom of Heaven." [11] Here is a creature who bears evidence of princely lineage in his erect carriage, inventive and artistic skill, and instinct to rule. Here is one with a brilliant future, destined to be God's vicegerent for the administration of this vast creation, if only he will look

[11] Matt. 19:14. This insight of Jesus contradicts the doctrine that the Image of God is completely destroyed in the human race by Adam's Fall, and children are born totally depraved.

up to his Father for guidance, and accept divine discipline of his heavenly potentialities.

2. The story of the Fall of Man in Genesis is a true parable of the *state of corruption* into which men always tend to fall when they begin to try out their God-given powers. The greatness of man's endowment is his undoing. His powers go to his head. He becomes proud and self-centred: "Ye shall be as gods" is the dream that subconsciously motivates his unbounded ambition. Thus exalting himself, he is cast down below the level of the beasts. The image of God, present in every child as he comes into the world, is overlaid and defaced as he acquires worldly wisdom and self-will. In the adult sinner it shows itself only in an irrepressible restlessness and anxiety that keep him wandering, wishing, complaining, seeking . . . he knows not why or for what. God takes pity on him, and sends prophetic messengers to coax him back to the parental abode, with threats and promises. Headstrong self-assertion and disaster, prophetic warnings unheeded and worse disaster; then, in the depth of affliction, prophetic words of encouragement, cries of repentance, and a great deliverance; so winds and winds and winds again the Eternal Road of God's dealing with mankind under the Law and the Prophets. Human pride and perversity are held in check by divine warnings and judgments, humbled occasionally by gratitude for great deliverances, but not radically overcome.

3. At last appears "the desire of nations," "one among ten thousand," the Man in whom the will to power is

utterly supplanted by the will to serve. In this Man, a selfless humility makes room for the divine Will to live at peace with his human will; through his freely surrendered human soul, the compassionate downreach of God's approach to man actually breaks through the insulating barrier of sin into fresh electric contact with lost humanity; and from this contact a new human race, standing in a new relationship to God, one of gratitude and humble dependence, begins to emerge. Creation need no longer groan and thrash about in restless travail; the "sons of God" are born at last! The members of the new humanity have ceased to dream ambitiously of being "as gods," and become really Godlike; i.e., humble and serviceable to their fellows as God in Christ has been humble and serviceable to them. Henceforth, God's search for man and man's search for the good life are merged. Man finds his chief end in serving the God who touches and redeems him in Christ.

Just *how* the conjunction of God and man took place in Jesus Christ, just *how* man's restless search for the good life and God's steady search for man at last met and merged, will always be a mystery. The initiative in this meeting must surely be ascribed to God; but without willing response on the part of the Man Jesus, no meeting could conceivably have taken place. In and through a true and willing human servant, God accomplished His eternal design and called His children back into fellowship with Himself. The last step in God's approach to man and the last step in man's hitherto halting and wayward response to God were taken in one and the same Person. In Christ "God and man have now become more at one than fife and drum," as the old Christmas carol says.

Centuries of acrimonious debate were devoted by the post-Nicene Fathers to the delicate problem of the relationship of the two natures, divine and human, in the Man Christ Jesus. The acrimony is the more regrettable when it is made plain that each of the two parties to the dispute persistently misunderstood the other, and neither party (except by occasional inadvertent lapses) was guilty of the subversive teachings attributed to it by the other.[12] But it is unlikely that so much heated debate would ever have been engendered by a purely academic issue. The issue of the relationship of the two natures in Christ is far from being an academic issue. In its practical meaning, it is essentially the issue as to *the kind of relationship between God and man which obtains in the new redeemed society of the sons of God*, of which Christians believe themselves to be members. Jesus is the Elder Brother of this society of the sons of God. The relationship between God and man in him is the type and pattern of what it ought to be and may be in us. The question is whether our communion with God is definable in terms of *ethical* oneness with God's *will*, or whether it involves a more intimate and *mystical* oneness, that transforms our very *being*. What was at stake in this great ancient controversy was something exceedingly practical: the nature of the Christian life.

[12] See the excellent study by Dr. R. V. Sellers, *Two Ancient Christologies* (London: S.P.C.K., 1940), pp. 202 ff.

The answer surely is that the Christian life at its best is always *both ethical and mystical;* both *obedience to God's commands* and *trust in His redeeming grace.*

Of course, the Church has never completely identified the new divine-humanity which she finds in her own life with the divine-humanity of her Lord and Head. Concerning him, the classic phrase is that "he was tempted in all points in like manner as we are, yet without sin." [13] It is clear that his Sonship is meant to be the type and pattern of our sonship, and the ardent expectation of the primitive Church was that through union with him we might become absolutely sinless; [14] but the sober judgment of the centuries has been that this does not follow. To adopt a striking distinction of Gerald Heard's, the majority of Christians are only more or less faithful "servants of God," somewhat intermittently at that! Above them is the level of life attained by the great saints, who may be called "friends of God," living pretty constantly the life of grace and faith and love. But it is the unanimous testimony of the saints that in the presence of Jesus, the unique Son of

[13] Heb. 4:15. The Epistle to the Hebrews is a very important testimony to the primitive Church's belief in the real humanity of Christ.

[14] I John 3:6, 9. This proves how powerful was the *mystical* view of the Christian life in New Testament times, long before the Church had any contact with Greek speculative mysticism. The Johannine "Thou, Father, in Me and I in Thee, that they also may be one in Us" (John 17:21) and the recurrent Pauline phrase *"in* Christ," are both genuinely mystical expressions in the New Testament. The logic of mysticism is always, "transformation into God's sinless nature by direct contact with God's power"; but *ethical* religion always continues to be aware of an infinite moral distinction between the righteousness of God and the righteousness of men. For a further discussion of the mystical and ethical elements in the Christian life, see Appendix C.

God, they feel like great sinners and cannot classify themselves as "sons of God" in more than a secondary and derived sense. Jesus is the head, they are only the members of the new humanity; he is the source from which grace streams in, they are the humble recipients and grateful transmitters of that grace. The union of God and man which is embryonic in them is full-fledged in him. Since most of us are not saints, we are not in a good position to question this judgment!

Great as may be our reverence for Jesus' unique Sonship, we must not allow ourselves to slur over his human limitations in such a way as to open up an unbridgeable gulf between his humanity and ours. He is the incomparable revealer of God to us, the incomparable example to us, just because he is surely one of us. New Testament criticism has done a great service in making it perfectly clear that Jesus' psychology as well as his physiology was fully human.[15] In countless ways, he shared the imperfect knowledge of his time; and he faced the mystery of the future with the same lack of detailed knowledge which makes us feel the solemnity of each New Year's Day.

Even his "sinlessness," the one point at which he

[15] Pittenger, in his recent book, *Christ and Christian Faith* (p. 19), points out that the limitation of Jesus' human knowledge was first definitely clinched in a clear example by Bishop Gore in his contribution to *Lux Mundi*. The example is Jesus' mistaken acceptance of the Davidic authorship of Psalm 110. Pittenger's whole discussion of the humanity of Jesus seems to me admirable, as is also his definition of the relationship between his deity and his humanity: "He is also divine, since his life as a total human act is supremely the instrument for God's action among men, and because through his human life with its consequences God's power and presence have been made uniquely real and available for man" (p. 79).

clearly towers above his followers, must not be conceived of in an inhuman way. Jesus was no marble
Apollo masquerading as a man, incapable of being
moved by the passions that drive us into sin. Nothing is
clearer in the record than that he was a very passionate
man, who spoke hot words in the heat of conflict with
his enemies, words which a cool historical critic, seeking a balanced judgment about the Pharisees and the
Sadducees, might have to censor at more than one point.
If Jesus had wanted to cultivate marble impeccability,
and avoid all possible criticism of his words and deeds,
he should have withdrawn from public life, and reserved his verdict upon his contemporaries until he had
achieved a balanced philosophic judgment upon them.
But he was not called to be a philosopher or a critical
historian, he was called and sent to save the world; and
part of his task in saving the world was to compel the
religious and civic leaders of his people to choose between joining him and opposing him — which had to
be done with hard, fighting words and deeds. The quality in him that was capable of doing this, while praying
for the forgiveness of his adversaries, was something
higher than negative sinlessness.[16] It was a goodness so
positive, so aggressive, that it tends to *destroy sin* and
create holiness wherever it strikes home. Jesus is not only

[16] At this point I find myself in disagreement with John Knox,
who admits Montefiore's contention that Jesus was unforgiving toward
his enemies, at least until the very last tragic moment on the Cross.
I should prefer to say that Jesus *fought* his enemies, and fought them
hard, for issues of transcendent importance; but was compassionate
and chivalrous toward them, and eager for reconciliation, throughout the battle. ("How often, . . ." Matt. 23:37.)

better than the best of his followers, he is their standard of goodness and their inspiration to be good — positively, contagiously, exhilaratingly good, not merely harmless, as so many good people are!

We have not said the last word about Jesus' relationship to the new humanity when we have described him as the head of the Church, and the source of goodness for its members. He is also the head of the whole human race, whether men know it or not, and his influence is destined to pervade all races, nations, classes, and institutions before it is done. Divine providence had already created in Israel a unique community, whose dogged loyalty to its covenant with God, facing martyrdom rather than disobey the least of His revealed commands, already represented a type of humanity which deserved to be universalized. But the new Israel, founded by Jesus and his apostles upon a new covenant sealed with his blood, broke free from all local particularities, and became at once, potentially, *the universal community of mankind under God*, capable (as its subsequent history shows) of penetrating divisive walls of partition, and drawing "all sorts and conditions of men" into one fold under one Shepherd. Buddhism is called a universal religion, and does contain many values that make a world-wide appeal; but it is essentially a religion for monks, and tends to destroy family and political life if fully universalized. Christianity is capable of preserving and hallowing all natural ties and constructive cultural activities, while drawing them all into relationship with the ordering will of God.

Only in our own day has the world become so fully one that the universality of Christ's headship can actually be tested on a planetary scale. If he is whom we believe him to be, he will not fail in this test. He will draw to himself the elect of all peoples, and through them exercise a redeeming influence upon world civilization. In the end, even nature will reflect his redeeming power, as the Apostle Paul foresaw. Nature today stands under a curse, blackened and scorched by man's belligerency, defaced and defiled by man's greed. The new race of which Christ is the head will not have finished its work until it has established a new relationship of reverence and loving care between God's human children and God's good earth. "The mountains and the hills shall break forth . . . into singing, and all the trees of the field shall clap their hands" (Isaiah 55:12). Yea, there shall be no more "dust bowls," no more "Black Country," no more "scorched earth."

III. *Jesus as the One who became the Living Christ*

Jesus might be described as the "head" and "founder" of a new humanity if he had merely furnished the Church with its "chief cornerstone," and determined the general lines on which the rest of the structure was to be built. This much he surely did. But actually, the relationship between the Church and her head has been more vital than any metaphor from the mechanic arts or the building trades can suggest. The Church has been the living, growing body of which he has been the animating soul, or, changing the figure, she has been the bride and he the husband. Nothing did more to create the Church in the first place than the conviction that Jesus had survived his Crucifixion and become, by his Spirit, *a living Presence at the heart of the Church*, "even unto the end of the world"; nothing has done more to keep the Church alive than the conviction that her Lord still lives, still guides, still intercedes, still works and fights in and through her for the enlargement of the new humanity.

It is not necessary to distinguish too sharply between the idea of the Living Christ and the idea of the Holy Spirit. The Holy Spirit was felt by the Early Church to be both the abiding presence of the Risen Lord, and the abiding presence of that divine power which had raised him from the dead. God sent Jesus, Jesus sent the Spirit, God sent the Spirit. In distinction from that *coming-forth to meet us* which is the special characteristic of God the Word (whether in "parts and portions" in the prophets or in its fullness in Jesus) the special characteristic of God the Holy Spirit is a kind of *bubbling-up within us* (*or among us*). The Spirit, or the Living Christ, is the most *immediate* and *inward* form in which we experience God. When we think of the inwardness of this experience, the way in which it fans to flame the spark of God that is at the depth of our own being, we speak of the Holy Spirit; when we connect it with its source, and the whole movement of redemption, we may properly refer to the Living Christ, for the flame in us is a flame kindled by Jesus,

and constantly replenished by the grace that comes
to us from the Word of Wisdom and Power that
was incarnate in him. The Living Christ is the Yea
to which the Spirit says Amen; the Yea and the Amen
both testify to the same unshakable promises of
God.

*Whether we describe this inward Presence of God in
the Church as the Holy Spirit, or as the Living Christ, it
proceeds from Jesus,*[17] *and is an extension of his life.*
Canon Quick has shown how disastrous are the effects
upon Christian thought of the tendency to isolate the
figure of the historic Jesus from the spiritual development
of the Church in succeeding centuries. When thought
concentrates (as in the Ritschlian school) upon the
isolated figure of the historic Jesus, it ends either in a
Unitarianism which minimizes the unique revelation of
God in him, or in a "Jesuolatry" which loads every con-
ceivable divine attribute upon his human shoulders. When
thought concentrates (as in the Hegelian school) upon
the development of the Christian movement, it ends
either in an idolatrous worship of the Church as she is,
or in a reduction of the Incarnation to a general embodiment of the divine Idea in man and nature.[18] To avoid
these and other grave deformations of the Christian
Gospel, we need to think, when we say "Christ," both

[17] In this connection, the famous *filioque*, whose addition to the
Nicene Creed was the occasion of the split between Eastern and
Western Christendom, is a matter of some importance. The Holy
Spirit proceeds not only from the Father but "also from the Son";
it is the Spirit of Christ as well as the Spirit of God.

[18] Cf. Quick, *Liberalism, Modernism and Tradition*, chaps. i and ii.

of the historic life of Jesus and of its continuation, through his Mind or Spirit, in the Church. The Christ who saves is this Christ, who once walked our human way amid all the difficulties we have to face, but triumphed over them all by God's power, and is "alive forevermore" in the midst of the Church.

In an earlier study,[19] I have underlined the danger of baptizing conventional morals and average churchmanship into the name of "Christ." I still think the danger a real one, but it is serious only when the idea of the Living Christ is allowed to drift out of connection with the actual life of the historic Jesus. Then, indeed, the name of Christ becomes a blank check for all our favorite clichés and prejudices. But if the real historic Jesus, or his real Spirit, is anywhere about the premises, he does not tolerate such forgery of his name! There is something in the very heart of the Church that is properly called the Mind of Christ, and this Mind acts as a sharp criterion of much that is called "Christian." John on Patmos saw the Living Christ standing in the midst of the Seven Churches of Asia with a two-edged sword of judgment proceeding out of his mouth, while at the same time he held the stars of their divine destiny in his hand. So it is still. Christ's Spirit is not only our Comforter, but our Judge and our Vindicator. This it is that is divine in the Church, that sifts and purges the poor human materials of which the Church is composed, and uses the faithful "remnant" that remains for God's own purposes, so that the gates of hell cannot prevail

[19] *A Psychological Approach to Theology,* chap. v, pp. 153-65.

against her. Churches can fall, but the Church of the Remnant never, for she is the chosen Body of the Living Christ, who is "God with us" still.

IV. Jesus as the One who shall come again

"We preach Christ Crucified, Risen, and Coming," said the big sign in front of a city church. When I saw the sign, I did not go in, for I concluded (I hope not unfairly) that the exposition of Scripture in that church would be drearily literalistic, and the Christ of Armageddon would have chased the Christ of the Beatitudes out of that pulpit. But it is tragic that I should have to draw such a conclusion, for every true Christian church ought to preach *the Christ who shall come* as well as *the Christ who once came* and *the Christ who abides with us*. All Christians ought to be adventists. All Christians would be adventists, if they carefully thought out the implications of their faith in the coming Kingdom of God. If they would only think out these implications, and make them a part of their public teaching, they would not be plagued so much with odd and fanatical adventist sects; for the man on the street has a shrewd and justified suspicion that the Bible contains a word of great comfort concerning the imminent coming of Christ into the world to which his morning newspaper refers; and if he cannot get such a word of comfort from authorized Biblical interpreters, he will get it from unauthorized sources.

The doctrine of the Second Coming of Christ means

essentially that *the work of God begun in Jesus of Nazareth is not yet complete, and needs further divine action to complete it — action which, when it takes place, will be recognized as the conclusion of the same divine drama which started with the Babe of Bethlehem in his Manger.* This drama has a peaceful beginning (The First Noël), a tragic counterplot culminating in the Cross, an unexpected turn for the better in the triumph of the Resurrection and the heroic Acts of the Apostles; but it is still in suspense. The Rule of God which Jesus came to restore is still in dispute; and in our time the opposition to God's sovereignty is actually gaining in power, annexing new territories right and left before our eyes. Unless God shall act again, sending forth His Son again at this historic crisis, as long ago He sent forth His Son at another great turning point of human history, it looks as though all that was achieved by the First Coming and the Abiding Presence might be undone! Without faith in a Second Coming, it is hard to retain faith in the First.

That is not to say that the Final Coming of Christ is now at hand. Two thousand years of Christian history, during which many crises have looked like Armageddon, should by this time have taught us patience and given us a far look into the future. The mysterious imagery of the Book of Revelation is dear to the Christian heart, and embodies our deathless conviction that, if not in time, then beyond time in the Ages of Ages, the "kingdoms of this world" shall at last become the Kingdom of our Lord and of His Christ. But this conviction should not lead us to interpret the present crisis as a proper occasion to don our ascension robes and wait on the housetops for the sound of the last trump, as the Millerites did a century ago. Rather, we should see in the present crisis a "type" or an "earnest" of Christ's Final Coming, corresponding to those Old Testament types and prophecies which led up to the First Coming.

Christian thought has always made much of what might be called a *periodic* return of Christ. Along with the thought of his finished work and his continued presence, the Church has cherished the thought of a fresh outpouring of his grace and power from time to time. In the rhythm of the Christian year, Christ's Advent is celebrated over and over again. Every year at Christmastime we pray with Phillips Brooks that the "Holy Child of Bethlehem" may "descend" and "be born in us today." We mean this in no merely commemorative sense; we believe that "where meek souls will receive him still, the dear Christ enters in" — freshly enters, to work a new work wherever he is so received. Yet this type of periodic return is so silent, so inward, that it is hardly distinguishable from a steadily abiding presence. Its rhythm is the heartbeat of the continuing life of the Church.

It is not enough, in such times as ours, to think of Christ's Advent so quietly and meditatively. In this time of world war and world revolution, apocalyptic language is needed to interpret the course of events. A European friend writes to me:

I am of those who feel that the present time has something of an apocalyptic depth and horror — and also grandeur. Something of the hidden meaning of history is uncovered as if we were given a foretaste of the final struggle between heavenly and earthly "powers and dominations." The spiritual struggle cuts through national boundaries and the entanglement seems to become more tragic every week. I know no better description of what we are going through than the 13th chapter of the Book of Revelation.

This is the chapter concerning the "beast" who was given power "to make war with the saints, and overcome them," and who caused all, "both small and great, rich and poor, free and bond, to receive a mark in their right hand or on their foreheads, that no man might buy or sell, save he that had the mark, or the name of the beast, or the number of his name" (Rev. 13:7, 16, 17). Many in our time have thought to discern behind the dark political forces that have risen to menace the world the veritable face of Antichrist. I believe they are right. Antichrist *has* come back; though he is not to be identified with any one man or nation. But Jehovah's Witnesses are also right when they announce that Christ has "returned to the Temple" to set up his "Theocracy." Both Christ and Antichrist have reappeared in the world today. Even through the roar of dive-bombers and the yells of human antagonists, the ear of faith can hear the sound of their spiritual combat filling all the sky.

The power of Antichrist springs from the weakness and unfaithfulness of Christ's followers. "Chesus vas not bad," said a young Jewess, on first reading the New Testament. "No, he vas *not* bad! He vas a gr-r-eat reformer. . . . But ven I zee his beoples, I am zorry for Chesus." The whole tragedy of modern Jewry — alienated by unchristian Christians from One who *belongs* to the Jews, and whom they could best interpret to the world — is contained in those simple words. But some non-Christians have less discrimination than this young Jewess; instead of being *sorry* for Jesus because of his people, they are contemptuous of him, and hate his very name. Eventually, they come to conceive of God in the image of Christ's antithesis; and so arises the power of Antichrist in our time. Consistent anti-Semites, who hate the Jews precisely because Jesus was a Jew, must, to be perfectly logical, try to erect a New World Order upon the negation of everything that Jesus stands for. When it comes to that — and it has come approximately to that, with Herr Rosenberg and others of the fanatical inner circle of Nazidom — then Antichrist seals his doom by exposing the ugliness of his unveiled countenance, and Christ "returns to the Temple" again, to claim the sovereignty of earth for God and for the humble.

It is still premature to announce that Christ has actually returned with power to our tormented world. Signs of His [20] approach are not lacking. In the Temple,

[20] I am using capitals in this last paragraph, for we have now reached a high point where we can see that we *must* use them. Christ now means for us: *the divine power and wisdom that created the world, that spoke in parts and portions through the prophets and philosophers, that entered into sacrificial union with lost humanity in Jesus of Nazareth, that continued to act in the Church by the Spirit, and that shall yet act more powerfully in the world at large when He finds more room in human hearts.*

there is a new penitence and a new yearning for His cleansing, even though it be done with a whip of cords. There is a new consciousness that it is not possible to serve Him comfortably and halfheartedly; we must either walk with Him along the *Via Crucis*, or stand with those who mock Him upon His Cross. The spectacle of the Confessional Church in Germany becoming a Church of the Catacombs, a church crucified with Christ, rather than to bow down before Antichrist, has stirred the whole Christian world to its depths; it brings back the courage to suffer into Christian veins where the blood of their martyred ancestors had grown thin and sugary. Whenever we are ready to live by Him and die for Him as Paul and Francis and Luther were prepared to do, He will indeed return with power. We are not ready, but we know more clearly with every new stage in this advancing world tragedy that there is none other to whom we can turn for deliverance. And so, in penitence and in longing, we pray the prayer that was oftenest on the lips of the primitive Christians, the prayer *Maranatha*, "Our Lord, come!" Knowing that it will cost us much to receive Him and give Him the room in our lives that He deserves, we still pray, "Even so, come, Lord Jesus!"

Epilogue for Non-Christians

THIS book was written for Christians, by a Christian. It aims to help restore faith in Jesus Christ to the central place which it rightfully holds among Christians, from which it has been removed of late, with disastrous consequences.

Nothing herein is meant to disparage the faith of Jews in their Torah, the faith of Buddhists in their Dharma, or any other honest faith in what is truly good and holy. That same wisdom and power of God which Christians find in Jesus, others find elsewhere; indeed, Christians themselves believe that the divine Word pervades all places and is accessible to all peoples.

Christians hold no monopoly of the divine Word, but neither do they hold a monopoly of Jesus. He is not their property; it was *to the world*, not to any privileged group, that God sent His Son. If, therefore, any non-Christian should listen in upon this Christian discussion, and find that the Christ here set forth belongs to him, and he belongs to Christ, let him not feel that to admit this is to capitulate to religious aggression, or be disloyal to his own religious heritage.

We who now are Christ's found in Him the completion and correction of our own religious quest of God — God whom we were seeking by many and various pathways, as the Christian fellowship is drawn from different peoples and divers cultural traditions. When, therefore, non-Christians find fresh apprehension of God in Jesus of Nazareth — and how can they fail to do so, if they get a good look? — it is their right to interpret that new knowledge of God as the completion and correction of their own religious heritage. If they can make Jesus revolve about some other center of divinity as a satellite, let them do so. Only it is our experience that God-in-Christ makes us revolve about Him as our center, by His own inherent gravitational pull, and makes us glad to do so forever and ever.

That is why we talk — as I have sometimes talked in this book — about the coming universal Kingdom of Christ. It is not that we are plotting to subjugate the rest of the world by force or stealth, and bind throngs of captives with ropes to our hero's chariot wheels. It is only that we have found ourselves so content to be His that we are sure He has the power to win His way peacefully and humbly with others, as He has with us. He is so utterly our Servant that we have no choice but to confess Him as our Master, and the world's future King.

Appendix A

The Relation Between Historical Criticism and Christian Faith

IF HISTORICAL criticism is a religious duty for Bible-loving Christians, how comes it that Bible-loving Christians have so often been exasperated with the Biblical critics, and cried out against them as enemies of the faith? The causes of this regrettable dispute are analogous to the causes of the long-standing dispute between natural science and natural theology, now happily in process of settlement. It is a dispute concerning the boundaries and relations between two kinds of knowledge that are at least relatively independent of one another.

Modern science got its start by resolutely eliminating all metaphysical questions about "final causes" from the realm of physics. This was legitimate and necessary; but it was illegitimate to conclude (as many scientific philosophers later did) that there was no room left for God or metaphysics, since science had "proved" that there was no meaning or purpose in nature. Actually, the ancient metaphysical judgment that nature's order and nature's very existence are grounded in a divine creative Power of some sort, holds as good today in Einstein's universe as it did in the universe of Aristotle and Ptolemy. This judgment is little altered by the mighty progress of modern natural science, and modern materialists have discovered few objections to it that were not already made by Lucretius. It may be excessive to say with Gilson that "the highest metaphysical problems in no way depend upon the answers given by science to its own questions" (E. Gilson, *God and Philosophy*, p. 120), but at least it can be said that the two orders of knowledge are relatively distinct, and control one another mainly in a negative way. Nothing can be true in metaphysics that is contradicted by some well-attested scientific fact; no scientific theory can be allowed to pass without scrutiny when it flatly contradicts some well-established metaphysical verity — usually because of some smuggled-in metaphysical assumption!

In the case of Biblical revelation, we are faced with an analogous distinction and relationship between two orders of knowledge. On the one hand is the historian's judgment as to "what actually happened," "what was originally meant"; on the other hand is the judgment of Christian faith which finds the Word of God in these historical events and through them learns to know its personal Lord and Master. As with science and metaphysics in their dealings with nature, so with criticism and faith in their dealings with the Bible, *the materials for judgment are the same, but viewed from two different angles*. Faith apprehends the eternal *in and through the historic*, the divine *in and through the human*, and so can never be *absolutely* independent of historical criticism. Yet faith-judgments are *relatively* independent of the results of criticism. The devout Christian, long before he becomes aware of critical problems in the New Testament, has formed a naïve but essentially sound faith-judgment about the central figure in the Gospels, whom he has also met as a living Presence in the Church. Confronting these Gospels, illuminated by the light of this living Presence, he cries, "*Here, here is my God, here is my Lord and Savior*, revealed more clearly in this one swift-moving current of events than anywhere else in the whole broad expanse of nature and history." How such a faith-judgment, leaping across centuries of time, may claim the title of "knowledge of God" or "personal acquaintance with Christ" has been very well discussed by John Baillie, in his doctrine of "mediated immediacy." (See *Our Knowledge of God*, pp. 178–98.)

Faith has already decided, then, in advance of historical criticism, that God is revealed in the Bible, and Jesus is my Savior. It is not within the competence of criticism to condemn this judgment of faith, but only to determine the precise course of events, the form and content of the documents, in which the revelation is given. Criticism trespasses on the domain of faith when it presumes to conclude that the Bible is just an ordinary book, or Jesus an ordinary man. Faith knows better, and rightly resents such presumption. On the other hand, faith trespasses on the domain of criticism when it presumes to conclude that the documents which contain the record of divine revelation must all be historically authentic, and the events must have occurred exactly as narrated. The religious meaning of events is often best brought out by dramatic foreshortening of history, or by legendary additions. So, for example, in Drinkwater's play, *Abraham Lincoln*, the historical facts of Lincoln's life are very freely handled. (Lincoln is represented as making a speech at Ford's Theatre, just before his assassination, in which phrases from the Second Inaugural are used.) But this falsification of history enables the author to bring out the inmost religious meaning of Lincoln's character in dramatically effective style. The Sermon on the Mount, the narrative of Passion Week, and many other passages in the Gospels are foreshortened in this way, while the miracle stories probably contain legendary additions. To what extent this is so is purely a critical question, with which faith has nothing to do, any more than with the problem of the composite authorship of the Pentateuch, or the literal veracity of the Chronicler's history of the Hebrew Monarchy.

That God revealed Himself in Biblical history, and supremely in Jesus, is a judgment of faith, like the judgment that the world as a whole has a divine Ground; *how* God's Biblical revelation has taken place and been recorded is the proper concern of the critic, as the process and order of God's creation is the proper concern of the scientist. When either faith or criticism steps out of its limited sphere and attempts to legislate for the other, it should be sent back within bounds. Theology, of course, must draw upon both, using each to correct and supplement the other.

Appendix B

The Historical Element in Christianity [1]

I

Christianity is historical in at least two senses: (1) it drives toward a historical goal, and (2) its message takes the form of a historical narrative, an "old, old story."

1. Not all religions drive toward historical goals. For the mystic type of religion that has generally prevailed in India, time is a wearisome, meaningless round, the "wheel of re-birth," and salvation consists precisely in *escape* from history. The Buddhist temples and pagodas which add so much to the loveliness of the landscape throughout the Far East are not meant to be lighthouses to guide men on their way toward distant historical goals; they are meant to be houses of refuge to which men may repair when disillusioned with life, sick of the social struggle, and hungry for the peace of a timeless eternity. The cryptic smile on the lips of the great stone Buddhas is half compassionate, half humorous: compassion for the poor victims so feverishly revolving the wheel of life like slaves in a treadmill; humorous contempt for the utter futility of the whole historical process. The

---

[1] An address given December 29, 1941, before the Association of Biblical Instructors, and later printed in the *Journal of Bible and Religion*. Reprinted here by permission. With addresses by Professor Brightman of Boston University and Professor Elliott of Union Theological Seminary, it was part of a symposium on the philosophical, historical, and functional aspects of Christianity.

way of salvation, for the Orient, does not lie onward and forward along the plane of history, but up and out into the Great Beyond that is impervious to time and change.

Christianity belongs to quite another type of religion, *prophetic* rather than *mystic*. Zoroastrianism, Judaism, and Islam belong to this same type. Although all four of these prophetic religions have imbibed a good deal of other-worldly mysticism from their Oriental or Hellenistic environment, their attitude toward history is fundamentally different. Mystical piety and monastic withdrawal, marked as they have been at times in prophetic religions, can never mean the same thing in this context which they mean in the context of a purely unhistorical religion. They do not mean deliberate desertion and final escape from the social struggle; they mean temporary retreat, in order to recover strength and perspective for renewing the battle. For history, to all prophetic religions, is, as William James would say, a "real fight," where great issues are at stake, and much depends upon the loyalty and valor of each participant. History is a drama with an intelligible plot, giving meaning to every new deed, while its denouement still remains in suspense, giving urgency and responsibility to each new decision. Prophetic religions, so long as they keep the true prophetic spirit, are always pressing forward toward new historic objectives.

It may be asked whether the goal of prophetic religion is definable in purely historical terms; whether its ultimate outreach does not involve some supertemporal goal lying beyond all temporal goals. It is true that most prophetic religions hold out the hope of heaven to their adherents, and think of the whole historical process as rounding off at last into eternity. But eternity as they conceive it represents rather the *fullness* of time than the *absence* of time; and one's eternal destiny depends not upon despising all temporal affairs, but upon faithful and humane dealing with such obviously temporal matters as food and drink and neighborly help: a "cup of cold water" to the tired traveler, a friendly lift to the wounded man fallen among thieves.

World-weariness is not unknown in prophetic religion, but the most religious men were long ago defined by Zoroaster as "those that make this world advance" (*Yasna* 30:9). John Macmurray is right: the idea of progress, though it be irreligious in some of its recent modern forms, could never have arisen save upon the soil of such prophetic religions as Judaism and Christianity. Greek thought, often credited with the paternity of this idea, was dominated to the end by the notion of eternal recurrence; it remained convinced, with Ecclesiastes, that "the thing that hath been is the thing that shall be, and that which is done is that which shall be done; and there is nothing new under the sun." (Eccles. 1:9 – a very Greek passage in the Hebrew Scriptures!) For faith in a really open future, hope of a really better world, we are indebted to the prophets of Persia, Arabia, and Palestine.

2. Prophetic religions not only drive toward historical goals, they also think of history as the great medium of divine revelation, and when asked what they believe about God, they *tell a story*. For Zoroastrianism, *all* history is the vehicle of divine revelation, for in all events is seen the persistent conflict of Truth and Falsehood, Right and Wrong, Light and Darkness. This does not cease to be true for the other prophetic religions; they all see God at work in the whole historical process; but they find the clue to the meaning of universal history in *specific chains of exceptionally revealing events*, to whose memory they cling with what Sholem Asch calls "obstinacy of recollection."

Judaism to this day obstinately recalls the story of God's covenant with Abraham, the Egyptian bondage, Moses the deliverer and lawgiver, the conquest of Canaan, the glory and decline of David's kingdom, the Babylonian captivity, and the re-establishment of the Temple and the Law under Nehemiah and Ezra. The sufferings of modern Jewry are set within that ancient framework of alternating tribulation and deliverance; so they can be understood, faced, and borne.[2] The same chain of events is treasured up in the Christian consciousness, but to it is added the story of the coming of the Christ "in the fullness of the time," His ministry of teaching and healing, His sacrificial death upon the Cross, and His glorious Resurrection, together with the Great Commission which He left His followers, to "make disciples of all nations" — memories which still largely account for the hopefulness and world-wide scope of the Christian movement.

It will be observed that the sort of history treasured up by historical religions is what Richard Niebuhr calls "internal history"; that is, history which is ours and which we believe in, as Lincoln believed in American history when he gave the Gettysburg Address, history which "calls for joy and sorrow, for days of rededication and of shriving, for tragic participation and for jubilees." [3] It is *history-with-a-moral*, never to be equated with mere objective history on the one hand or with everlasting moral principles on the other. Objective, scientific history is not the foe of internal history, for it is of the essence of historical revelation that it actually happened, once upon a time, as the life of Jesus actually happened in the days of "Caesar Augustus" and "Pontius Pilate." But mere objective history can never take the place of internal history; for the events of objective history are finished, dead and gone, whereas internal history is the continual re-enactment of the past in the present — as at Christmastime we pray that the "Holy Child of Bethlehem" may be "born in us today." This re-enactment is possible

---

[2] See the noble book of sermons to Jewish refugees by Rabbi Ignaz Maybaum, *Man and Catastrophe* (London: 1941).

[3] H. Richard Niebuhr, *The Meaning of Revelation*, pp. 60–68.

because there is a quality of universality in these events, a capacity for endless repetition with endlessly fruitful consequences; but it would never do to extract universal principles from the events, and then forget the events. No, it is necessary to remember these events, brood over them, philosophize about them, experiment boldly along lines that they support; for there is a presence of God in them which is dissipated and lost when they are replaced by abstractions of any sort. Internal history is the collective memory of the ongoing religious community; if the Christian Church should ever lose its historical consciousness it would be like a man stricken with amnesia, wandering aimlessly because with the veiling of his memory he had lost all sense of direction and purpose.

Internal history is best expressed in mythological terms. That is not to say that prophetic religions can ever use mythology as mystical religions do, to body forth in a story that which never happened in time, and never *could* happen in time, because it is essentially timeless. Prophetic myths are *actual history, dramatized and simplified to bring out its enduring meaning and ultimate issues.* So the history of the kings of Israel and Judah is dramatized and simplified in the books of Samuel, Kings, and Chronicles, to bring out the point that it goes well with God's people when they remember the Law and the Covenant, and ill with them when they forget. So also the story of the life of Jesus is dramatized and simplified in the Gospels, to bring out the point that He is the one foretold in Old Testament prophecy, sent and anointed to save His people from their sins.

The foundation of actual history is clearly visible in such passages of Scripture, and the labors of historical critics only serve to reassure us, periodically, that these were real events and great events, *deserving* to be exalted into historical myths for the instruction of all posterity. The historical element is not so apparent in the mythology of Creation and the Fall, with which the Old Testament opens, and the Christmas myths, with which the New Testament opens; but I would venture to assert that such obviously *unhistorical myths* as these nevertheless contain *the distilled essence of historical experience*, and give precious clues to the meaning of the actual history which underlies the whole Biblical narrative. The prophecies and apocalypses with which the Old and New Testaments close are also made of historical stuff. They express historical wisdom in imaginative pictures of the future, which help us to act decisively in the present. Neither bare historical facts nor mystical allegories of eternal truth could possibly do for us what imaginative myths based on historical experience are capable of doing.

II

Let us now consider the relationship between this *historical* element in Christianity and the *philosophic* and *functional* aspects of Christianity. The relationship will be clarified, I think, if we raise two objections against the historical interpretation of Christianity, one from the functional angle and one from the philosophic: (1) Can a historical religion be functionally flexible when it faces new historical situations? and (2) Can a historical religion ever escape from local and transient particularities, so as to become universally valid, as the philosophic ideal requires?

1. We are all aware of the fact that historical traditions are sometimes extremely inflexible, especially when religious veneration has sanctified certain ancient words, ceremonies, beliefs, institutions, and made it seem an impiety to propose the slightest alteration in them. How unfortunate that religious veneration for the Book of Genesis should make it impossible for traditionalists to adapt their minds to the acceptance of new knowledge about the early history of the earth and the descent of man. How tragic that faith in the literal veracity of the Book of Revelation should lead

some contemporary traditionalists to face the crisis of the twentieth century with a millenarian mentality unchanged since the first century. How urgent the necessity of overcoming the inertia which keeps each of our denominations inflexibly attached to its own special traditions, and unable to unite in the face of a common emergency.

One proposed cure for this traditionalistic hardening of the arteries which periodically threatens the life of historical religions is set forth in Professor Coe's *What Is Christian Education?* Coe recommends that less stress should be laid on the *transmissive* function of Christian education, and more stress be laid on its *creative* function. With the contention that the Christian movement should come freshly to grips with every fresh difficulty that crosses its path, and think creatively about new social situations instead of trying to inculcate traditional maxims derived from other social situations, I am in hearty agreement. I might even go so far as to suggest that in every generation some school of Christian thought needs to make up its program and credo out of strictly contemporary materials — as Gerald Heard did when he wrote *The Third Morality* — in order that contact with the problems of each age may be vitally maintained. But I am sure that unless other schools of Christian thought, and prevailing practice in Christian education, maintain a strong emphasis upon the transmission of precious traditions and old, old stories, Christianity will become *less* creative, not *more*, in consequence of severing its connection with its prime sources of inspiration and guidance.

One of my psychological colleagues has been carrying on a series of experiments with monkeys whose frontal lobes have been dissociated from the rest of their brains by a surgical operation. At first it appears that such monkeys are not affected at all; for no one of their normal functions is destroyed by this operation, whereas if certain other sections of their brains had been dissociated, the function of sight, hearing, or locomotion might have been eliminated or badly crippled. Upon prolonged observation, however, it becomes evident that these animals have suffered a serious loss. They have lost the capacity to bring past experience creatively to bear upon the solution of new problems. There is still a carry-over from past to present in the form of stereotyped habits, and this is sufficient to solve certain problems of a somewhat mechanical sort; but what is missing is that very thing which in a human being would be characterized as creative imagination or adaptive intelligence. On the basis of such experiments, I think it might be said that a Christianity which became purely functional and utterly unhistorical would actually function less flexibly, less adequately, less creatively than one which continued to carry on transmissive education, and so faced the new contingencies of the present with the aid of great pattern-ideas derived from past history. *An unhistorical Christianity would be, so to speak, a Christianity lacking its frontal lobes.*

A certain student, after reading a good deal of John Dewey's philosophy, and jumping to some hasty conclusions about its meaning, once wrote me a paper in which he declared that his philosophy of life was *not to have a philosophy of life.* Every life situation was so utterly different from every other life situation, he explained, that if you adopted any fixed principles or attitudes it only cramped your style, and prevented you from recognizing the uniqueness of each new event as it came along. *Pure experimentalism,* or *trial-and-error behavior,* he said, was what Dewey's philosophy required; i.e., to do in each life situation whatever seemed best at the time. The reference to "trial-and-error behavior" helps to define the meaning of this "pure experimentalism" somewhat precisely. The behavior of a rat in a psychological puzzle-box is known as trial-and-error behavior; but after the rat has bumped his nose a few times or got a few electric shocks, his behavior tends to become more effectively intelligent *exactly in proportion to his ability to bring past experience to bear upon present problems.* A rat who remained a pure experimentalist, and never used his historical sense, would be an unusually stupid rat, learning nothing from his errors and his trials. May we not conclude, then, that extreme experimentalism in religion would fail quite as badly as extreme traditionalism — though of course in a different and opposite way — to solve the problem of adaptation to new circumstances? What is wanted is *such a use of historical revelation as is really relevant to present needs.*

2. Let us turn, then, to the philosophic difficulty about the lack of *universality* in historical religion. It is a very real difficulty, especially in such an age as this, when universality appears to be the *sine qua non* for any religion that hopes to deliver the human race from its present distresses. Our planet has become so small, and so unified in an external sense, that there is now a pressing demand, for the first time in world history, for spiritual unity on a planetary scale. All the great historic religions have to be re-examined in the light of this situation; and the first question that arises in the course of such re-examination is whether *any* historical religion can possibly develop into a world faith without sloughing off its local and provincial elements; i.e., everything that ties it to a particular historical tradition. The pride and partisan bias of all racial, tribal cults of "blood and soil" obviously excludes them from the possibility of becoming the universal faith of mankind. Is it otherwise, we ask, with those so-called "universal" religions which, in spite of their humane and generous aspirations, continue to demand loyalty to particular historical leaders and particular historical traditions as the test of genuine discipleship? Can Christianity ever become truly universal while it continues

to insist that all men must be baptized into the name of Jesus — a particular historical character who lived two thousand years ago?

Philosophic reflection can certainly do much to purify historical religions of their accidental and nonessential elements, and bring their universal elements into clear focus. It does so by enunciating general truths whose validity can be appreciated and tested by all men of good will, whatever their traditional background and special allegiance may be. It is unlikely, however, that universality in the religious realm can ever be attained by the process of abstract generalization alone. Actually, the process that has led us as close as we are to universality is one in which concrete historical movements and warm personal allegiances have played a decisive role. It was not through a gradual philosophic broadening and mellowing that Judaism became Christianity, but through a particular historical movement that was at first tragically divisive in its effect — "not peace but a sword." The Leader of this movement has now proved His ability to cross all sorts of national and cultural boundaries, and draw to Himself all sorts and conditions of men — not imperialistically, but through love and humility. Those who follow this Leader see in Him God's own universal justice and all-comprehending mercy, made flesh and continuing to work in our midst, even unto the end of the world. To renounce allegiance to such a Leader, in favor of some hypothetical spiritual center about which the world's life might be organized, would be to prefer the shadow of universality to its substance. In so far as the words and deeds of Jesus are merely relative to a past historical situation, it is of course idolatry and partisanship to take our stand upon them. But in so far as they are indeed the wisdom and power of God, drawn nigh unto us for our salvation, they must be rebroadcast by all to whom they effectively come home, precisely in the interest of the final religious unity of mankind. Loyalty to Christ is not the destruction of philosophic universality, but its concrete fulfillment.

The practical corollaries of all this can be very briefly stated. Christianity cannot be effectively taught unless its history and classic literature are fully and adequately presented. The mastery of objective historical data is not in itself enough, however. History must become *internal* history before it can be an adequate vehicle for the transmission of Christian faith. It tends to become internal when grasped in its dramatic or "mythical" significance, when treated as the embodiment and illustration of philosophic ideas, and when used as a storehouse of suggestions for the creative handling of contemporary problems.

The philosophic and functional treatment of the Christian faith is thus a necessary supplement to its historical treatment, and vice versa. It must be so, if Christian faith in God is on the right track: a God revealed in history, decisively revealed in the character of the Christ, but pressing on to new victories in each new historic era, and aiming to comprehend His children in one universal Family. To desert the Great Tradition of Judaism and Christianity, just at this juncture when it is so violently assailed on every hand, would be treason to humanity. It would carry the human race back to the "beggarly elements" from which our primitive ancestors started out aeons ago. But the Great Tradition cannot be defended unless it is constantly renewed. Two excellent means of renewing it are to keep it constantly open to philosophic interpretation and criticism, and to reapply it constantly to the solution of new functional problems.

The Creeds of Nicaea and Chalcedon

A PERSONAL statement about my attitude toward these influential creeds may be in order.

I came to my study of them prejudiced on the whole
against them. Unlike the Roman Catholic, Eastern Orthodox, and Anglican churches, whose respect for these creeds
seems sometimes almost to imply their verbal inspiration,
the Baptist and Congregational churches (with which I
have been affiliated) are suspicious of *all* creeds, save as
temporary and convenient statements of living faith. No
theological language ever carries so much weight, in these
churches, as does the language of Holy Scripture; and in
the Baptist churches, it is always possible to shelve any proposed denominational creed by moving to "reaffirm the
New Testament as our only creed."

To this initial prejudice against creeds in general, I must
add an unfavorable first impression of the whole period in
church history from which the Nicene and Chalcedonian
creeds came. Worldly ecclesiastics scrambling for power
and prestige, and willing to unite upon a formula of concord only because the emperors insisted upon church unity
as a means of preserving political unity in their domains —
how could religious truth emerge from such a secular background? And specifically, in the case of the Formula of
Chalcedon, Pope Leo's famous letter to Flavian, known as
"The Tome," which swung the Council and determined the

decision at Chalcedon, seemed to me to be based upon a false
and misleading interpretation of the facts of Jesus' historical
career, now thoroughly exploded by New Testament criticism. To draw up a list of completely human aspects in
Jesus' life, and parallel it by a list of completely divine
aspects, as though our Lord were continually shuttling
back and forth between two opposite and incompatible
roles, seemed to me the very *worst* way to go about a study
of his divine-human character.

To allow for a fair criticism of these initial prejudices and
unfavorable first impressions, I have read three relevant
books by Anglican authors: *Liberalism, Modernism and
Tradition*, by Canon Quick (Longmans, Green, 1922), *Two
Ancient Christologies*, by R. V. Sellers (S.P.C.K., 1940),
and *Christ and Christian Faith*, by Norman Pittenger
(Round Table Press, 1941). All three books have deepened
a growing recent conviction of mine that in spite of all the
quarrels of worldly ecclesiastics, it was a truly Christian
religious consciousness that actually prevailed at Nicaea and
Chalcedon. This religious consciousness is found in a more
classical form in the New Testament itself; but the New
Testament faith needed to be articulated into a clear,
orderly theology, and *the main line of fruitful development
in Christian theology passes straight through Nicaea and
Chalcedon.*

I am glad to find that Canon Quick does not hold that the
dualistic philosophy underlying the Christology of the
Nicene and Chalcedonian councils is unconditionally valid
without adaptation to modern knowledge, but only that
this "traditional" view is sound in its main outlines, and
constitutes a needed corrective to the two views that have
recently prevailed: the "liberal" Ritschlian stress upon the
historic Jesus, and the "modernist" stress upon the Christ-
idea, both tending in opposite ways to identify God and
man too simply and too irreverently. This tends to indicate

that the Nicene and Chalcedonian formulas are at least *negatively* true, as safeguards against certain recurrent extremes of thought which they decisively rejected in their own day, and which the Christian consciousness always will reject when it becomes aware of their implications.

But Dr. Sellers seems to me to go farther at this point than Canon Quick, and prove that these formulas are *positively* as well as *negatively* true. That is, he indicates that they sprang from a great religious consensus which underlay all the apparent differences of the Alexandrine and Antiochene Christologies. They represent not merely a tactical compromise between two actually irreconcilable views, but the statement of a rich paradoxical union of two aspects of truth which all important Christian groups held in common, and which never can be separated except by a violent effort of abstraction: the so-called "mystical" and the so-called "ethical" schools of thought, which Harnack separated in order to cast his vote pretty exclusively for the latter, but which were both present in the theology of Irenaeus, and have been united in the main line of Christian thought ever since.

Antioch, with its Jewish background, tended to emphasize the *ethical* aspect of the Christian life, *moral obedience of the human will to the divine Will*. From this point of view, one must sharply distinguish the divine Will which commands from the human will which obeys, and be very jealous of the full and true humanity of Jesus our great Example, who "learned obedience by the things that he suffered." Alexandria, with its Hellenistic background, tended to emphasize the *mystical and metaphysical* aspect of the Christian life, the real and inward *communion*, the mysterious transforming *fusion* between divine grace and human nature, to which every "twice-born" Christian soul can bear witness. From this point of view, one must insist that the unity of God and man in the new humanity (and in Jesus its Founder) is something more intimate than that external conformity involved in moral obedience to God's commands. Without inwardly cleansing and transforming grace, it is impossible to obey God's commands. In Jesus, the gracious God has drawn so near to us that He has become, as the mystics say, "nearer to us than we are to ourselves," and we have become to Him "as a man's own right hand is to a man." His nature has become so joined to ours that our nature is made more and more Godlike, in so far as it is possible for mortal men to be like God.

Both of these emphases had characteristic dangers and difficulties — which were constantly pointed out by the opposing party. Alexandria was in danger of destroying the distinction between finite creatures and their infinite Creator, encouraging mortal men to believe that by "eating God" in the sacraments and practicing mystical exercises they might literally become human gods, or so one with God as to be pantheistically absorbed in Him. Antioch was in danger of reducing Christianity to a new legalism, encouraging men to suppose that by strong will power, following hard upon the footsteps of Jesus, they might earn the right to adoption as sons of God by their own efforts, without any transforming, cleansing infusion of divine grace.

Actually, each school of thought rejected these extreme apparent implications of its position, and stood for what we may call *ethical mysticism* as the true nature of the Christian life; i.e., a life of deep mystical faith-union with God in Christ, looking not toward *absorption* in God as its goal, but toward an active ethical life of love toward God and fellow men — mystical and metaphysical union with God as the *root* of a transformed life, whose *fruits* are the ethical "fruits of the spirit" described by the Apostle Paul. This conception of the Christian life carried with it a conception of the "two natures" in Jesus substantially at one with the famous formula of Chalcedon: in Him, and ideally in His Church, God and man are united "indivisibly and inseparably," as the school of Alexandria contended; but they are likewise "unconfusedly, unchangeably" distinguished from one another as Antioch insisted they must be to preserve the ethical quality of the relationship.

I feel particularly indebted to Norman Pittenger for clearing up my difficulty about Leo's "Tome." He shares my objection to the " 'stop and go' relationship of divinity and humanity, with first one and then the other appearing and performing its proper functions" (p. 25), but he points out that *if* this be the correct interpretation of Leo's meaning (which Canon Quick doubts) the "inseparably" and "indivisibly" in the Chalcedonian formula tend to rule out any such view, and the development of theology since Chalcedon has made it increasingly clear that "the Incarnate never leaves his Incarnation" (p. 26).

It has greatly intrigued me, moreover, to discover how constantly Mr. Pittenger's Christology, which is aware at every moment of the authority of Nicaea and Chalcedon, duplicates the results of my own less technical approach to Christology. I deliberately refrained from reading his book until I had practically finished writing my own, but when I did so I found that we had arrived independently at similar conclusions. There is no better way to clarify my precise meaning in my final chapter than to refer theologically trained readers to Mr. Pittenger's book. It is written in an idiom that is different from mine, with constant meticulous awareness of the heretical shoals to right and to left, defined by the ancient Fathers. I have not hitherto thought it worth my while to familiarize myself with all these sandbanks in any such detail; but having tacked about in this same channel in my freer, more simple-minded way, I can testify that these shoals are there, from having scraped upon them myself! Once again, from this unpremeditated meeting of my mind with Mr. Pittenger's, I am led to classify myself as a liberal Catholic in the Evangelical Protestant camp. And though I still prefer the language of Scripture to that of Nicaea and Chalcedon, I now believe that these and other creeds of the Church Universal clarify the meaning of Scripture in valuable and important ways.

Index